PRAISE FOR
FROM LOST TO FOUND

"I have told women for years that Nicole is the kind of gal I am so grateful is leading our generation. She is wise and compassionate; plus she's honest, and her words are filled with hope. I have no doubt you'll feel led and loved well by God through her words, and I have no doubt this book will change your life in the best ways. Thank you, God, for Nicole, and thanks, God, for your truth! Give us ears to hear."

—JESS CONNOLLY, BESTSELLING AUTHOR OF
YOU ARE THE GIRL FOR THE JOB

"This book is what we are all looking for every day of our lives—a road map to freedom. So many of us find ourselves stuck in darkness, feeling around for a way out. Through Nicole's incredible story, study, and insight, she offers that way out, pointing us toward the greatest light and freedom there is—Jesus."

—JEFFERSON BETHKE, *NEW YORK TIMES* BESTSELLING AUTHOR
OF *JESUS>RELIGION* AND *TO HELL WITH THE HUSTLE*

"As a marriage and family therapist and as a woman who has lived the words she writes, Nicole teaches from the trenches, daring us to reimagine what it *really* means to be blessed. Through biblical wisdom, vulnerable personal narrative, and psychological insights, she illuminates an unlikely path to healing, showing us that when we release the defenses we once trusted in order to feel valued and safe, we find ourselves open to God's transforming grace."

—JONATHAN MERRITT, CONTRIBUTING WRITER
FOR *THE ATLANTIC* AND AUTHOR OF
LEARNING TO SPEAK GOD FROM SCRATCH

D0055137

"A beautiful story of breakthrough with powerful insights that will help you move from hurting to healing. You will love Nicole's honesty, wisdom, and helpfulness as she leads you on a journey to find emotional wellness."

—MIKE FOSTER, AUTHOR OF *YOU RISE GLORIOUS* AND HOST OF *FUN THERAPY*

"*From Lost to Found* is the book I wish I had on my nightstand during my own season of struggle with fertility. With the warmth of your closest friend and the wisdom of your most trusted resource, Nicole holds nothing back as she reminds us of the growth that springs from unexpected circumstances and the beauty there is to be found in the wake of what has been lost. Take your time and let the truths in this book settle deep. *From Lost to Found* will leave you comforted, challenged, and changed."

—HEATHER AVIS, BESTSELLING AUTHOR AND NARRATIVE SHIFTER

"*From Lost to Found* is an important work for anyone who has ever tried to prop up her life with accomplishments, security, and comfort—which is pretty much all of us. This gorgeously written story is much more than a bunch of pretty words strung together; this one is going to set women free."

—JENNIFER DUKES LEE, AUTHOR OF *IT'S ALL UNDER CONTROL*

"Maya Angelou once said the most important virtue was courage, as it was necessary to all other virtues—to be giving, loving, and kind. Nicole Zasowski's example of courageously finding her fears and giving them over to the lessons of faith is more than an inspiring story; it is, in short, a devotional guide to the fruits of the Spirit and becoming a loving follower of Jesus. Read and follow her lovely example."

—TERRY HARGRAVE, PhD, EVELYN AND FRANK FREED PROFESSOR OF MARRIAGE AND FAMILY THERAPY, FULLER THEOLOGICAL SEMINARY

"So many things make this spectacular book stand out. To begin, Nicole is a highly skilled and sought-after therapist, so the truths woven into this book spring from a deep well of professional knowledge and biblical wisdom. But because Nicole is both a gifted storyteller *and* a woman who intimately knows the loss and the hope about which she writes, this book reads like you're hearing from a longtime and loyal friend who understands where you've been and what you need to hear to keep growing. But best of all, Nicole wraps all of this in the good news of the gospel and shows us just how free we *really* are to be found in Christ alone."

—JEANNIE CUNNION, AUTHOR OF *MOM SET FREE*

"If you have ever tried to find your identity in more striving, performing, and achieving, this book is for you. If you have ever tried to white-knuckle control your life into the perfect picture on the outside while you were crumbling on the inside, this book is for you. And if you are ready to give up your grip on comfortable for the deeper, more meaningful places God is calling you, this book is definitely for you! In this important and necessary book, Nicole gives us the permission to come undone to everything we think defines us—these boxes we keep checking that only leave us feeling emptier—so that we can find true freedom that comes on the other side of letting go."

—MARY MARANTZ, AUTHOR OF *DIRT*, SPEAKER, AND HOST OF *THE MARY MARANTZ SHOW*

"*From Lost to Found* is a unique gift in that Nicole, a licensed marriage and family therapist, not only offers her expertise on emotional health but also vulnerably takes us along on her personal journey from pain to emotional freedom. This book is for anyone stuck in a cycle of pain, longing for emotional freedom, or (already) deep in the process of changing patterns and behaviors (like me). With the wisdom and practical steps found in these pages, coupled with God's ever-present help and grace, you're equipped to begin on the path to freedom. Spoiler alert: joy and peace are not the destination; they are welcome companions in the process."

—TRINA McNEILLY, AUTHOR OF *LA LA LOVELY: THE ART OF FINDING BEAUTY IN THE EVERYDAY*

"*From Lost to Found* hits us all between the eyes as we deal with the reality of how we struggle with control. Nicole's vulnerability and honesty are key in how we can be honest with ourselves, allowing God to give us the freedom to be who he has called us to be. Don't miss this wonderful read!"

— **CHERYL SCRUGGS**, HOST OF THE *THRIVING BEYOND BELIEF* PODCAST FOR WOMEN

"Nicole's story of losing and finding is both hers and all of ours. She reminds us—beautifully—that sometimes what we assume is an ending may actually be the seeds of a sacred beginning. Thank you, Nicole, for bravely opening your hands so we might learn to trust the mystery of surrender."

— **LEEANA TANKERSLEY**, AUTHOR OF *ALWAYS WE BEGIN AGAIN*

GIVING UP WHAT YOU THINK YOU WANT

FROM LOST TO FOUND

FOR WHAT WILL SET YOU FREE

Nicole Zasowski

W PUBLISHING GROUP

AN IMPRINT OF THOMAS NELSON

Published in Nashville, Tennessee, by W Publishing, an imprint of Thomas Nelson.

Author is represented by The Christopher Ferebee Agency, www.christopherferebee.com.

Thomas Nelson titles may be purchased in bulk for educational, business, fund-raising, or sales promotional use. For information, please e-mail SpecialMarkets@ThomasNelson.com.

Any Internet addresses, phone numbers, or company or product information printed in this book are offered as a resource and are not intended in any way to be or to imply an endorsement by Thomas Nelson, nor does Thomas Nelson vouch for the existence, content, or services of these sites, phone numbers, companies, or products beyond the life of this book.

Unless otherwise noted, Scripture quotations are taken from the Christian Standard Bible®. Copyright © 2017 by Holman Bible Publishers. Used by permission. Christian Standard Bible® and CSB® are federally registered trademarks of Holman Bible Publishers.

Scripture quotations marked NIV are from the Holy Bible, New International Version®, NIV®. Copyright © 1973, 1978, 1984, 2011 by Biblica, Inc.™ Used by permission of Zondervan. All rights reserved worldwide. www.zondervan.com. The "NIV" and "New International Version" are trademarks registered in the United States Patent and Trademark Office by Biblica, Inc.™

Scripture quotations marked ESV are from the ESV® Bible (The Holy Bible, English Standard Version®), copyright © 2001 by Crossway, a publishing ministry of Good News Publishers. Used by permission. All rights reserved.

Scripture quotations marked NKJV are from the New King James Version®. © 1982 by Thomas Nelson. Used by permission. All rights reserved.

Scripture quotations marked THE MESSAGE are from *The Message*. Copyright © by Eugene H. Peterson 1993, 1994, 1995, 1996, 2000, 2001, 2002. Used by permission of NavPress. All rights reserved. Represented by Tyndale House Publishers, Inc.

ISBN 978-0-7852-2645-1 (e-book)
ISBN 978-0-7852-2643-7 (TP)

Library of Congress Cataloging-in-Publication Data

Library of Congress Control Number: 2019032522

Printed in the United States of America

20 21 22 23 24 LSC 10 9 8 7 6 5 4 3 2 1

For Jimmy: I would choose you in any story.

CONTENTS

PART 3: BREATHING IN: FINDING A LASTING PEACE

PART 4: LOOKING UP: CHOOSING JOY OUTSIDE OF CIRCUMSTANCE

FOREWORD

It was not just any bracelet.

It was orange and made of leather, soft but strong.

And across it, in gold, the letters *BELIEVE* were attached.

The bracelet passed between two friends, handed off in church or mailed overnight. It was wrapped with care and sent with a note.

But the bracelet needed no other words. It said it all.

It was often received with tears and then wrapped around a wrist belonging to a heart that needed a reminder—a reminder that we must choose to believe even in the storms.

The bracelet was an anchor, an embrace from a friend who could not be there in person but was there in prayer.

The author of this book—my sweet friend Nicole Zasowski—and I have passed that bracelet back and forth numerous times.

Though we have shared with each other this one word—
BELIEVE—I was delighted to receive *From Lost to Found*, a
book full of words that will bless you with the same gifts Nicole
has long blessed me with in friendship. She is an excellent lis-
tener; I know that as you walk through these pages, you will feel
as if she is a good friend offering you a trusted ear.

Nicole presents gentle truths about how the loss of what
you've dreamed about becomes your path to being found. It is a
journey she shares intimately and intentionally. She generously
reveals her hardships in order to point you to how God will place
purpose in your heart despite your pain.

Nicole invites us to examine seasons of disappointment or
waiting and leads us to understand that God will generously
loosen our grip off of anything we hold more dearly than Him.
She demonstrates how He will generously carry us through our
suffering and rescue us from our aspirations if they are not in His
will. Nicole shows us what it looks like to practice gratitude in
the midst of loss and how, when we do so, joy is found and self
is lost—a sweet reversal.

My hope is that you not only read this book but pass *From
Lost to Found* on to a friend—just like the bracelet Nicole and I
have shared with each other across the miles—as a reminder to
believe.

—ELISABETH HASSELBECK

DAUGHTER OF A KING, WIFE, MOM,
AND AUTHOR OF *POINT OF VIEW*

INTRODUCTION

AN UNLIKELY PATH TO HEALING

This is the book I could have easily written for someone else—anyone but me. One of my greatest joys as a marriage and family therapist is helping my clients discover their significance and security outside of circumstance. In that role I am very comfortable offering truths for them to apply to their lives. But the real truth is that I was not yet brave enough to live these truths for myself.

I couldn't see that I was missing out on the peace and joy that I was so passionate about helping others find. I had no idea that behaviors I have used to protect myself from pain since childhood—behaviors like shame, performing, and control—only numbed the broken parts of myself that desperately needed healing. I lived my life from the deep belief that peace and joy can only be found on the far side of a dream realized, a change of venue, or a goal achieved.

But the behaviors that once served to protect me against pain in my early years became barriers to meaning and connection later in life. It was not until I confronted loss and intense pain that these protective behaviors failed. Here, I discovered for myself what I knew to be true for my clients: the unlikely path to healing begins when we release the behaviors we once trusted and find ourselves with empty hands. Only empty hands are open to receiving what we need in the transforming reality of God's grace.

I also used to think that the enemy keeps us enslaved only by making us miserable. But I'm learning that one of the ways the enemy holds us captive is to make us comfortable without Christ. He gives us the illusion that the good life is a self-constructed story in which we are at the center, instead of a God-breathed story of grace in which we are transformed and called to empty ourselves to those around us. I envisioned Christ's pursuit of me as a rescue from unwanted circumstances. But sometimes God's rescue looks like prying our fingers off what we think we want so that we can receive what we need.

This is not a book about how to look on the bright side or how to search for the silver lining in the cloud. It is a story of how God took my loss and wove into it His story of redemption, which provided me with an essential and beautiful transformation.

From Lost to Found is divided into four parts that help us identify (1) what we are losing, (2) how our reactive behaviors are failing us, (3) what joy is there for us to find, and (4) how we can move forward by choosing to walk in the freedom God has for us. At the end of each of the four sections are discussion questions that will help you process these ideas in the quiet of your own heart or in groups of trusted friends. Because here's the good news—God is writing a story of redemption in your life too—one that offers the same transformation I found.

As you journey with me through my story, my prayer is that you will find your own. I pray that you will do the difficult but worthy work with me as we discover the healing that we need—to give up those things you think you want for what will truly set you free.

PART 1

CALLED OUT

THE PAIN OF LOSING WHAT WE THINK WE WANT

CHAPTER 1

CALIFORNIA
LOSING COMFORT

We are far too easily pleased.
—C. S. Lewis

A text message alert burned blue on my phone, catching my glance from the corner of my office. The light was easy to spot in the small, windowless room. With tan carpet and a beige couch to match the walls, the room and everything inside it was the color of chewed bubble gum.

"Annie left."

The phone suddenly felt heavy in my hands. My fingers hovered over the screen as I struggled with how to respond. *What to say?*

3

The red light glowed above my office door, abruptly announcing the arrival of my next client, my last appointment of the day. A reply would have to wait.

My client wasted no time pouring out her story. But I was distracted as I thought about my own story—one that was changing without my permission or direction. Between concerned nods, mm-hmms, and how-does-that-make-you-feels—the basic building blocks of counseling conversation—the two words tumbled around in my mind. *Annie left.*

I began to chew on those words and wrestle with the meaning of them. No matter how I put the puzzle pieces together, hoping for a different picture at the end, the picture was the same every time. Our life was changing without my consent. My husband's colleague Annie had left her job, and her position was now open on the other side of the country.

Ever since Jimmy began his career as an intern at ESPN, he had dreamed of joining its business strategy team. There were three potential positions that would make this career move possible. One was in Los Angeles, where we currently lived and where I was content to stay; another was in New York City, where I might consider living. (I had always fancied myself the kind of girl who could pull off a New York chapter.) And then there was one in Connecticut, where I could never imagine living. The thought of moving across the country to a small town with limited career opportunities for me (or so I thought) made me feel stuck and claustrophobic. Annie, of course, had held the position in Connecticut.

"See you next week," I said, forcing a smile and leading my client out the door. As I watched her walk across the courtyard toward the parking lot, I wondered how many more weeks I would meet with her and all the other clients in my practice, which I had worked tirelessly to build under the license of a supervising therapist.

I took the long way home.

Why is this happening?

It was a question with an answer I was not ready to hear.

I rolled the car windows down and let the hot May air breeze through, drying my runny nose and tear-soaked face as I scanned the radio for a sad song. This melancholy moment needed a soundtrack. I savored the smell of the orange trees lining the street, which was appropriately called Orange Grove Boulevard.

Though I never considered myself much of a California girl, I had come to love living in Pasadena. I did not have bleached-blonde hair. I had absolutely no interest in learning to surf, and even after six years I still found palm trees and Christmas lights an odd combination. But in that moment, I couldn't imagine living anywhere else.

Jimmy and I had met as undergraduates at Pepperdine University and had been married in Malibu on the ocean shore, just down the street from campus. Only days ago we had signed the lease on our first real, non-student apartment. We had walked the movie-perfect streets of Pasadena neighborhoods and selected all our favorite houses, and though it was probably unrealistic, we dreamed of calling one of them our own someday. Pasadena promised everything we hoped for in our life together.

I loved California, but I loved how I felt in California even more. We had a close community of friends, a church where we felt a sense of belonging, and mentors who poured into our lives. I had a job I loved and had built a reputation for myself. Moving felt like a threat to everything that was important to me.

There was always the possibility that Jimmy would not get the position. But he had a long list of impressive qualifications and admirable qualities, despite his humility. I just knew he would land the job. Later I would learn that the Connecticut business strategy team had specifically called him and asked him to apply, which was a strong indication that the position was his if he wanted it.

Also, I had a sinking feeling that this move was just as much for me as it was for Jimmy. I couldn't articulate why, but the mere possibility of moving across the country was already highlighting the comfort of my current circumstances. Life was easy and came with a lot of props. And though I don't believe life needs to be difficult to be worthy, I hesitantly wondered if my comfortable life held securities that kept me from the wrestling and working that leads to growth. Though I was unwilling to fully admit it to myself, the move was not something that I wanted, but I was afraid it was something I needed.

I pulled into the parking garage of our building, and my feet mindlessly traced the route to our apartment. I stepped into the loft, and Jimmy hugged me. No words were necessary. He knew the weight of his news. After more silence than either one of us was accustomed to, he asked if I wanted to walk to Starbucks. Bless his heart. Starbucks usually cured all for this Seattle-grown girl. This was something that could not be fixed with a caffeinated beverage. But craving the reassurance of routine, I agreed.

On our usual walk down Lake Avenue, I felt a deep nostalgia as I noticed all our familiar haunts with each passing block—Trader Joe's, the Coffee Bean, and the local frozen yogurt shop. Arriving at Starbucks, I glanced across the intersection and spotted the retro Pie 'n Burger sign crowning the tiny fast-food restaurant, a famous Pasadena landmark. We had never been to Pie 'n Burger, and I did not particularly care for pie or burgers, but I suddenly felt very attached to the old establishment. Leaving Pasadena would be a sad goodbye.

We paced back up Lake Avenue, drinks in hand. Between pregnant pauses, I asked questions I didn't really want to hear the answers to. Where would we live? What job opportunities existed for me? Would we stay in Connecticut forever? What are Connecticut people like? How would we connect and find community? Almost all of the answers were, "I don't know."

But these questions were not the questions I was *really* asking. Though I could not articulate the source of my anxiety at the time, what I really wanted to know was how I could be relevant when I had to leave my connections, established reputation, and accolades behind. It wasn't leaving California that made me fearful. I was scared to leave because my sense of worth and security were tied to the life I had built and the praise I had received as a graduate student and therapist in Pasadena. I couldn't take them with me. My discomfort revealed the unsightly fact that my significance was very much in the perfect image I had created instead of the person I was created to be. How could I be enough without a life that proved it?

I wasn't afraid of the unknown; I was terrified of not *being* known. For me, leaving my home meant leaving my identity behind.

These feelings and behaviors were not new. Despite having parents who loved me well and valued me for who I was, I had worn this deep fear of inadequacy like a tattoo ever since I could remember. No crushing devastation or trauma led me to believe that my worth hinged on my performance. Rather, my arrival at this conclusion had been subtle and slow. As the oldest of three girls, I possessed a certain bravado and know-how that lent itself to a reputation of being strong, capable, and responsible.

I sustained a tremendous work ethic from an early age, which (with a few exceptions) often led to success and praise. And I loved the praise. It made me feel significant and secure. So much so that I began to wonder who or what I would be without it. Underneath my successes, strength, and capabilities, I lived with the dread that I might be exposed as ordinary and unremarkable. Good enough wasn't good enough. So decorating myself with accolades and titles and working harder than everyone else around me became necessary for my emotional survival.

I avoided disappointment at all costs out of the strong conviction that experiencing disappointment would mean that *I* was a disappointment. As a result, I became close companions with shame, performance, and control the way that some people become good friends with red wine and Netflix in their pain.

WHEN I AM CONFRONTED with a painful situation, I most often feel deep inadequacy followed by insignificance and then rejection. These have become my deepest wounds—forever raw like the skin underneath a scab.

My work as a marriage and family therapist has taught me that not all of our pain looks the same. Your story, and the feelings you carry as a result, might be different from mine.

My professor and mentor from graduate school, Dr. Terry Hargrave, trained me well in the therapeutic model he developed called restoration therapy. This process has taught me to listen for messages that clients receive about their identity and sense of safety as they tell their stories.

Some of the messages we receive are positive; they let us know that we are loved, unique, worthy, empowered, and not alone. Others are painful or confusing—damaging statements about our personhood and our sense of security in the world, which form the wounds we carry forward. Maybe you could never depend on someone to be present for you in the family you grew up in, and when you feel emotional pain you experience the sharp pang of abandonment or insecurity. Or maybe your environment was chaotic, and as a result you feel powerless and out of control. Or no matter how hard you tried, "it" was never good enough, and you carry with you a profound sense of inadequacy and a fear that you will never be able to measure up. Maybe you heard these messages from outside your home. Or perhaps the messages that cut you most deeply came from inside the four walls of your house. Maybe it was a tragic event that let you know the world was not safe, or the cutting words of another communicated a destructive message about your significance.

These messages shape the feelings that are particularly sensitive and painful to us. To survive them we develop ways of protecting ourselves—behaviors that are understandable but ultimately harmful to our relationships with ourselves and other people.

In his book *Restoration Therapy*, Hargrave outlines the four main ways we tend to cope with our pain.[1] Some of us might get angry and blame other people for the pain that we experience. Others of us might turn inward to shame ourselves and beat ourselves up for all the things we should do differently and all the ways we could be different. Some of us might attempt to control the world around us, ordering other people and events into place in an attempt to feel more secure. Or we may seek escape, shutting down emotionally or numbing ourselves with behaviors like watching television, drinking alcohol, sleeping, or shopping—whatever helps us forget the pain, even if only for a moment.

The wounds we experience and the reactions we employ are not who we are, but they do describe how we feel and what we tend to do when we are in emotional pain. Though these behaviors could be described as our brain's way of attempting to protect us from the feelings we find most painful, in reality they serve as barriers to experiencing a life of intimacy and abundance. Often these behaviors were necessary in order to survive the pain of our circumstances growing up and the feelings that followed. But as we grow and become adults who desire to take responsibility for our life choices and ourselves, these behaviors tend to get in the way of meaning and connection.

The enemy wants us to believe that this protected way of living is all there is—that the life we create for ourselves here on earth is as good as it gets. He wants us to focus on making a name for ourselves instead of using our gifts to glorify the name of God. The enemy is constantly tempting us to choose comfort over the calling God has placed on our lives.

Until we moved across the country, my reactive behaviors of shame, performance, and control had worked for me, successfully keeping me from the pain I dreaded most. Or they *appeared* to be working. As was the case with every transition in my life, I had felt insignificant when I arrived in Pasadena a few years prior, so I had shamed myself before others could reject me, and I had performed my way into a position where people were impressed by me. I was an old soul behind a young face, and I worked hard to prove that I was competent. I formed connections and studied vigorously so I could feel confident in my therapeutic skills and avoid the feelings I dreaded most: inadequacy, insignificance, and rejection. I worked odd hours to build a practice that would exceed the expectations of my superiors. The shame, performance, and control seemed to reward me with the life I wanted and the love and security I deeply craved. I had built a life that made me very comfortable but protected from peace and joy. I knew where I lived, but I had forgotten where I belonged.

Now God was asking me to leave that life and my decorations behind, and I had no idea who I was without that life or how I would feel safe in the unknown of this next season. Moving to a place where I had no job, no contacts or connections, no community, and no home meant facing the question of who I was apart from my performance and the praise of others. And the crushing truth was that if I were to be honest with myself, I would have answered, "I am *nothing*."

EVERYTHING WENT AS WELL FOR JIMMY as I expected. A few weeks after that text message, we made the decision to move to Connecticut. I graduated from Fuller Theological Seminary with a master of science in marriage and family therapy in mid-June, closed down my practice, and said goodbye to too many beloved friends in July. By August we were gone.

I moved with a resolve to build my comfortable life all over again. The mere idea made me bone-weary, but I knew no other way. My survival strategy was less a conscious plan of attack than an emotional reaction to my deep fears of being exposed as ordinary and not enough. I would build my image one impressive feat at a time. I would make an impression that would win people over. And I vowed to work harder than anyone else to feel at home in Connecticut. Home was where I felt valuable and secure, and I knew no worth or safety apart from the kind that is earned, proven, or built with my own efforts.

But this time it wouldn't work. The strategies I employed my whole life were about to fail me—over and over again. I had no idea that this move was just the start of a season that would pull entitlements from my grasp and leave me with empty hands to hold something entirely new.

No one tells you that being comfortable is the worst thing that can happen to you. I was not looking to be rescued from the life I always wanted and worked hard to achieve. But I had been dreaming dreams that were too small and was content with a life I could make with my own two hands. This comfortable life was about as helpful and wise as treating cancer with anesthetic. My way of living only kept me numb to my need for healing.

Sir Francis Drake is thought to have once prayed the prayer I didn't know I needed in those California days:

> Disturb us, Lord, when
> We are too well pleased with ourselves,
> When our dreams have come true
> Because we have dreamed too little,
> When we arrived safely
> Because we sailed too close to the shore.
>
> Disturb us, Lord, when
> With the abundance of things we possess
> We have lost our thirst

For the waters of life;
Having fallen in love with life,
We have ceased to dream of eternity
And in our efforts to build a new earth,
We have allowed our vision
Of the new Heaven to dim.

Disturb us, Lord, to dare more boldly,
To venture on wilder seas
Where storms will show your mastery;
Where losing sight of land,
We shall find the stars.[2]

Though I didn't pray this prayer then, God was gracious to disturb me anyway. One might assume that a fresh start elsewhere would be the cure to my faulty thinking and reactive ways of living. But as it turns out, struggles travel across state lines. A move across the country was only the beginning of God's merciful disturbance in my life.

CHAPTER 2

A HEART DIVIDED

LOSING SECURITY

*It's a good thing to have all the props pulled out
from under us occasionally. It gives us some sense
of what is rock under our feet, and what is sand.*
—MADELEINE L'ENGLE

For me, first days are difficult. They are wrought with unknowns and expectations that may or may not be met. And they're often accompanied by a pressure to prove myself. This first day was no exception.

On my first morning in Connecticut, I woke up squinting as the sunlight pierced our bedroom window. Window treatments were now at the top of my list of things to get in our new home.

Still half asleep, I rubbed my pulsing temples. Migraine headaches were usually my insistent companion during any kind of transition.

With no job, I had nowhere to be. And with our boxes still en route from California, I had nothing to busy myself with at home. I did, however, have an important agenda for the day. A colleague and friend from California happened to be visiting New York City that week. Though I had only said goodbye to her last week, something felt novel about connecting in a new place, so we agreed to meet for lunch in Bryant Park. It would be my first opportunity to navigate the Metro-North train line that ran from several towns in Connecticut into Grand Central Station.

I managed to put my feet on our bedroom floor, wincing in pain, blood rushing to my throbbing head. A train whistle blew outside, announcing an arrival at the Green's Farms train station. I had failed to fully appreciate the proximity of the train station to our bedroom window when we agreed to rent this guesthouse—a feature that some Realtors might reframe as "a commuter's dream." In addition, we were also situated right next to I-95 with nothing but a small marsh in between. We could check the traffic from our bathroom window.

I was grateful for this home, in spite of its quirks. It was six hundred square feet, falling well within the range of the qualifications for a tiny house. The owners' design motto when renovating the place must have been, "When in doubt, paint it white." In some places it looked as if white paint served a more functional purpose in filling holes and repairing other small defects. Nevertheless, as a couple who is generally afraid of color when it comes to decorating our spaces, we liked white. The home had a charming kitchen that opened up to the living space and a bedroom with an adjoining bathroom that was clearly designed for one.

We were told that this guesthouse was a speakeasy in the 1920s. We could still see the subtle line that ran along the living room wall (even with the many layers of white paint), indicating the place the bar once stood before the space was converted to a home.

The other rental options in our price range led us to feel especially grateful for this home. One apartment we toured had noticeably slanted floors. If you placed a ball at one end of the kitchen, it would roll to the other side with no assistance whatsoever. The kitchen also boasted an avocado-colored stove right in the middle of the floor; it had been advertised as a kitchen island.

Apparently real estate agents are not permitted to comment on things like school districts and crime rates. But as we stepped outside after viewing the house with the slanted floors, our real estate agent strongly suggested that we get in touch with the local police department to better understand the crime rate in other areas compared to this one—which helped us feel very confident our tiny, white guesthouse was the place for us.

Determined not to miss out on the chance to have lunch with a familiar face, I got dressed and made the three-minute walk to the train station just in time to board the 8:49 a.m. train bound for Grand Central. I felt ill but still found the train ride an entertaining experience.

A middle-aged man seated across from me asked a younger, hipster-looking guy for directions to Rockefeller Center. The passengers who overheard his question smiled condescendingly, leading me to believe that the answer to this man's question was obvious, and that in the greater New York City area, at least, there is such a thing as a stupid question. The woman seated next to me was singing and dancing along to whatever beat was blaring inside her large headphones. Her moves looked like one of those long, skinny inflatable characters outside of a car dealership, but she danced with the confidence of a Super Bowl halftime performer. A man seated directly behind me was talking loudly on a business call. The irritated looks on the faces of the people around me told me that this was a train *faux pas*. My first Metro-North train ride was proving to be quite an education. Spoken or unspoken, there were rules you were expected to follow.

Despite the distractions, I could not ignore the fact that my headache was getting worse. I made a concerted effort to focus my gaze out the window in an attempt to fight off waves of nausea. As the tunnel grew dark, signaling our approach to Grand Central Station, I began to sweat, and I could feel my stomach shaking its contents loose.

The train awkwardly chugged to a stop, and I wondered whether I could make it to a bathroom or, at the very least, a trash can. The doors opened, and I was immediately confronted with the smell of hot garbage. It turns out even a trash can was ambitious. I shoved my way off the train just in time to vomit all over track 25. Thankfully, New Yorkers have a focus and a drive that prevented them from taking much notice. There are few things that would surprise someone who lives or works in Manhattan, and I was grateful that no one seemed to pay much attention to me.

Bryant Park was closer than I anticipated. I found a bench in the shade of a tree that was almost as green as my face. I had arrived early and decided to spend the extra time scrolling my phone looking for jobs and orienting myself to the idea of being an "East Coaster." But as my thoughts wandered, the therapist part of me could not be ignored, and I became my own client. I started wondering about the deeper feelings that were causing me to become so anxious.

It was no coincidence I was feeling sick on my first day living on the other side of the country. This was developing into a pattern in my life. My first day of college orientation began with the campus police escorting me to the health center because of my severe stomach pain. There was something about the beginning of a new season that caused me to physically react by becoming anxious to the point of getting sick.

Anxiety is commonly referred to as a feeling, but my counseling training taught me to see it as a reaction or a secondary emotion—a mere symptom of a deeper wound. I had learned to see anxiety as a clue that I am feeling a deeper pain and believing a lie about my identity or sense of security. *What lie am I mistaking for truth? What feeling is igniting my nerves?* I thought. I quickly realized that my fears were very much related to my dreams and expectations for this next season.

OUR DREAMS FOR OUR LIVES can be fertile ground for anxiety to grow. Our minds easily run ahead toward our visions for the future, and the gap between where we are and where we would like to be can leave us feeling as though we are living on a live wire of worry. We fear that what we hope for will never be. We feel disempowered to turn our dreams into realities. We worry that we will be disappointed by our own futures. And we wonder what it will mean for our personal value if we fail to realize our dreams. These fears revealed the treasures of my heart:

success, notoriety, and the need to be impressive and be liked by everyone.

Of course, not everyone treasures the same things. But we can begin to discover and understand the treasures of our heart when we ask ourselves these questions:

- Where do our minds wander when given the space?
- How do we choose to spend our time?
- What keeps us up at night?
- What gets us out of bed in the morning?
- Where do our resources go?
- What do we most yearn to be added to our life?
- What are we most afraid will be taken away?

The answers to these questions can be helpful hints into our gifting and calling. But when our answers become our treasures—the hinges of our joy—they become idols. And we can serve only one god.

The Greek word for anxiety is *merimnao*, and the literal translation is "to be divided."[1] When I first learned this, I thought it meant that we become anxious when we are over-committed or when one part of life interferes with our ability to focus on another. But I now wondered if *merimnao* was less of an external problem to be managed and more of an internal matter of the heart. What if it wasn't my schedule but my heart that was divided? What if my motivations and the objects of my affection were divided in a way that was causing me to become anxious?

The story of the Tower of Babel from Genesis 11 illustrates the perils of a divided heart. Noah's descendants were living in Babylon, and though they spoke one language, their hearts were divided. Their most prized treasures and securities were invested in their own self-achieved greatness instead of in God. They wanted to build a tower that would reach the heavens and make a name for themselves. Their foolish aim was to place themselves in a position where they would not need God. God was far from being the one source of their actions and the single object of their affection. God became angry at their pride and arrogance and lack of dependence on Him. So He caused them to speak many languages, creating confusion that prohibited them from completing the tower.

This confusion sounded a lot like my own bewilderment and anxiety that day. I could see a division of my motives and object of worship. I was one day into a new chapter in my life, and instead of God being the only source of my actions and efforts there, I was focused on pleasing and impressing the new culture around me. Instead of seeking to serve God with my gifts and calling, I was building my own tower of significance by looking for a validating job and attempting to make a stunning first impression. I was seeing myself carefully observe my new environment, alert to the expectations of others, eager to please. But maybe having the props to my security pulled out from under me was going to become an opportunity to listen for the one voice that matters and to learn to stand confidently on solid ground.

Maybe the secret to security is not something that can be earned or manufactured from the outside but is making God the one source of our actions and the only object of our worship. Was it possible that my worry was a gracious clue that I, too, had not been willing to make Jesus the *one* treasure in my life? Perhaps my anxiety was a product of trying to serve the idols in my heart.

I now know there *is* another way. Though it is wise to seek wisdom from others, you only have to listen to one voice: the voice of your Father who knows your past, present, and future story. You only have to be one thing: the person God created you to be. You only have to follow one person: Jesus. You only have to live for an audience of One. And you only have to live the one life that you were made for and called to. These are answers that simply cannot be found outside of the promptings of your heart and the intimate conversations between you and God.

WATCHING NEW YORK'S LUNCHTIME CROWD pepper Bryant Park's manicured lawn that day, I wondered what it would feel like to tune my ear to one voice and to follow one God. What would I have to gain by giving up the pile of treasures in my heart? The mere question seemed to grant me permission to relax my shoulders and breathe more deeply.

I spotted my friend walking toward me from across the park—a scene that looked like a page from one of those Where's Waldo? books from my childhood. Just seeing someone who looked familiar seemed to ease the pain and nausea. Some treasures from California would always be worth keeping. But maybe not all.

CHAPTER 3

A WEDDING INVITATION

LOSING COMPANIONSHIP

> *The quest of the Inner Ring will break your hearts*
> *unless you break it.*
> —C. S. LEWIS

On most of those early, empty days, I found myself at a local coffee shop called Espresso NEAT in the nearby town of Darien. The rhythm of this daily appointment with myself provided a sense of structure. I reported for duty at the two-top table in the corner nearly every day, typing flurries of words and hoping to organize the feelings that were firing off inside me. My activities alternated between journaling and job hunting. Occasionally, when the view of my computer screen grew old, I would people watch, intently studying the Fairfield County folks as if I were tracking migration patterns in the Amazon.

The revolving groups of people were the same each day. In the early morning, businesspeople rushed in and out, slurping the excess liquid off the lids of their drip coffees, trying not to spill it on their suits as they rushed to make the early morning train to Manhattan. Often they started the workday on their cell phones in the shop. I never understood much of what they were saying, but they always seemed to take themselves quite seriously. In the midday hours, PTA committee moms discussed the perils of raising teenagers while somehow finding a way to boast about their own kids. Occasionally, the conversation would shift to house renovations, college admittance, or the next vacation. They were usually dressed in athleisure, but they never looked sweaty. And in the late afternoon, squirrely after-school kids wandered through the door in large groups, eyes cast down toward their phone screens—together but not.

One element was consistent across all these groups. Almost every person I saw wore an expression that I recognized to be loneliness. It was easy to identify a feeling that beat so strong inside myself. I also noticed that these customers seemed to enjoy talking with the baristas, often continuing their conversation from the day before in ongoing dialogue throughout the week. Customers' faces would light up like neon signs when the baristas would remember their names or ask for an update on something that was happening in their worlds that week. It was as if these four walls defined the one space in their lives where they were recognized for who they are instead of what they do—a place where they could belong without having to prove themselves worthy.

While fascinating, my observations were also discouraging.

I have heard it said that one can feel most alone in a crowd of people. I have also heard people refer to New York City as the loneliest city in the world. Crowds without connection mean nothing to our loneliness. I was comfortable being by myself and often relished the opportunity to have a few hours to sit with the company of my own thoughts. But being in a crowd only highlighted the fact that I was here but not seen. Nobody recognized me. No one walked into the coffee shop and was excited that I was there. Nobody knew my name or my story.

In the absence of conversation with another human being, loneliness became my closest companion. Nobody on the East Coast knew that pumpkin pie was my cake of choice for my birthday in August. Nobody recognized the name of where I went to graduate school. Nobody knew that both of my childhood best friends were named Megan. Aside from when Jimmy came home in the evenings, I had no outlet for talking about the deeper parts of myself. I had not yet formed relationships strong enough to hold my fears, my insecurities, my dreams for the future, and the ways in which I was trying to grow. So I just stuffed them inside.

It was not as if most of the people I met were unkind. I was at our new church every time the doors were open and felt hopeful about the relationships that were starting to form there. But history requires time to create. You can't make old friends. Or so I thought.

I felt as though I was in the waiting room but hadn't yet been invited past small talk and into people's everyday lives and the deeper parts of their stories. Trust is built with time. So the kind of relationship where you have permission to ask the tough questions and speak truth into each other's lives remained on the horizon for me. As I watched groups of people gather in this coffee shop, I wondered if I would ever be invited to the inside of one of those circles. Worse, I was afraid I might have to prove myself worthy before getting there, which sounded both painful and exhausting. And unlikely.

I felt so different from most of the people I encountered. In theory, I knew that pain is pain, no matter what it looks like, and that we all share the same emotional needs as human beings. But Fairfield County was one of the wealthiest counties in America. I now lived in a place where *summer* and *lunch* were verbs. Some of the things that appeared to matter here, I didn't have. I loved my college experience, but I didn't graduate from an Ivy League, as it seemed everyone else had. Jimmy loved his work with ESPN, and I valued my calling as a therapist, but neither one of us worked in finance. We liked our town, but we lived farther north on the train line than most people in Fairfield County, putting us farther away from New York City because there were more housing options in our budget.

The coffee shop crowd was an accurate cross section of the Fairfield County population. The differences I observed made it easy for me to assume that it would be impossible to connect and that I would never belong, as if the only things that go together are things that match. There was no dramatic rejection. I had not even made an attempt to connect. I merely watched and listened to the people around me day after day and decided that I was, and would probably continue to be, alone.

To be clear, I longed to be invited into someone's circle—to be given permission to step into the inside. But the differences left me worried that I would not be interesting to anybody and that I was not worth pursuing.

On one particular day, a girl named Paige walked into the

shop. She and I had been introduced a few weeks prior at church, and I saw her quite often at Espresso NEAT, as she was newly engaged to the director of coffee there—a dark-haired, cold weather–loving guy named Kyle. As director of coffee, Kyle was responsible for sourcing and roasting the coffee and overseeing the basic quality control of both the coffee and the preparation in the shop. I didn't know either of them very well, and most of our conversations had been limited to their upcoming wedding, but I liked Paige and Kyle. There was something about them that felt steady and safe, and I hoped we would become closer friends.

Paige smiled and waved at me as she bounced by. I smiled and waved back. It felt good to be recognized. She chatted with Kyle in the back of the shop, and I returned to journaling and job hunting.

I was engrossed in a half-written cover letter when suddenly a cream, parchment-textured envelope with "Mr. and Mrs. James Zasowski" scripted on the front slid across my line of vision and onto my laptop keyboard. I looked up to see Paige grinning. I almost couldn't trust what I was seeing. *Is this what I think it is?*

She picked up the wedding invitation, pressed it into my hands, and, looking a little shy, said, "I know we haven't known each other very long. But I just feel like we are going to be great friends. We'd love for you to be there."

Stunned, I stood up and hugged her tight for a long time.

"We'll be there," I managed to say, wiping a tear out of the corner of my eye.

"Great," she said as she bounced back to Kyle, who looked up at me across the shop. I smiled and mouthed the words *thank you*, seemingly unable to let go of the invitation.

It was a strange and wonderful feeling to be invited before I was known. In my world, wedding invitations were reserved for those who had played a starring role in at least one season of your life. They are given to people you would call when life unravels and you're confronted with a kind of pain you don't even have a category for. You send wedding invitations to the people who have danced with you in the light and helped guide you through the dark. Your guest list consists of people who have stood in the gap to pray when you didn't have the words or the strength to do it for yourself. Because weddings are expensive and the cost of each guest is high, it seemed reasonable to me that invitations would be distributed to those who had *already* demonstrated this kind of friendship.

JESUS MADE A HABIT OF INVITING PEOPLE first, of including people before they were qualified. In Luke 5, we read about Jesus gathering His first disciples. He told a skeptical Simon, whose fishing nets had come up empty all day, to let his nets down in the deep water once more. Simon argued but eventually complied, and when his nets became loaded with fish, he threw himself at Jesus' feet and told Jesus that he was not worthy to be in His presence. And Jesus simply told Simon to not be afraid and asked him to follow Him. There was no list of requirements or accomplishments to achieve. There was no burden of proof for Simon to carry. All he had to do was accept the invitation.

God has extended this same radical welcome to us through the person of Jesus. When Jesus conquered death on the cross, He rose with an invitation in hand, a saved seat, and a place of belonging for each of us. He established our value and reserved our place. The cross fulfilled our deeper need to be seen and our longing to belong to Someone who never leaves us on the outside looking in.

Knowing you are chosen by a God who has purchased your ultimate belonging won't erase the loneliness. God is an inherently relational being who created us in His image. Thus, we are made for relationship with God and with other people. But this is what I've learned the hard way: knowing we have been pursued by Jesus allows us to become the pursuer of others. Rather than waiting to be asked or hoping to be included, you can be the inviter. You can reach out *from* a place of significance instead of *for* your significance. And when you do, I think you'll find that you appreciate the differences between yourself and those around you that once made you feel excluded and afraid. You'll find a connection built with strength instead of pure neediness. You'll find some of the sweetest friendships you've ever known. You'll find that loneliness can actually pave the road to intimacy.

THE ENVELOPE I HELD IN MY HANDS that day argued against the assumptions I had made about being alone in Fairfield County. It appeared that the only person who was drawing circles was myself. I felt excluded without realizing that I had excluded myself. I had seen ways I did not fit in, and I had decided that I did not belong. I made quick judgments about people's characters based on the small window of what I could see, rejecting them before they could reject me and reinforcing my loneliness.

I stared at my name printed in scripted font on an invitation I didn't see coming and wondered if I had been getting it backward. I was waiting to be pursued by others in order to feel significant. But what if I was waiting for something I already had? What if knowing our inherent significance allows us to be the pursuer of human connection that we all crave? Maybe losing my narrow ideas about friendship would allow me to pursue a different kind of companionship—richer, deeper, and circle free.

I packed up my things and waved goodbye to Paige and Kyle from the front of the shop. I walked out the door, facing my life outside the four walls of Espresso NEAT. I looked one more time at the invitation for the January wedding, grateful for the reminder of my secure belonging without the burden of proof.

As it turns out, Paige was right. We did build a close friendship. But I will always remember that the invitation came first.

CHAPTER 4

WHEN YOU'RE CALLED

LOSING APPROVAL

Perhaps only when human effort has done its
best and failed, would God's power alone be
free to work.

—CORRIE TEN BOOM

I felt my hands shaking as I struggled with the clasp of my neck-lace. I was anxious about my 11:00 a.m. coffee appointment and felt it would help to look like a young lady who was from the East Coast. Or at the very least like a young lady who knew what the East Coast expected of her. The string of pearls my parents had given me for my eleventh birthday seemed appropriate.

I stood in front of the mirror, pressing my floral sundress

smooth with my sweaty palms, my hands pausing over my belly—still flat after months of trying to conceive. I felt like the only woman in Fairfield County who did *not* want a flat stomach. I fluffed my hair awake in spite of the humidity, my pulse racing. An acquaintance from my neighborhood back in Seattle had offered to connect me with a therapist she knew in the nearby town of Westport. The woman was the director of a group private practice, and she happened to be looking for a therapist to fill an opening she had on her staff.

The job appeared to be similar to the one I had left behind in California and was everything I hoped to find here in Connecticut. The woman had invited me to her home for a conversation over coffee. The conversation was not meant to be an interview, but I was nervous nonetheless. I wanted this time together to go well and was hoping this coffee hour would lead to an unofficial job offer. But more than that, I was hoping she would hear my story and believe in me. I longed for this woman to really see me—my personality, my heart, my vision, my mission—and I wanted her to love what she saw and be willing to fight for me. I guess I was looking for the approval of someone I deemed important and successful. Maybe she could give me the confidence that I, too, was important and had what it took to be successful in Fairfield County.

I pulled the idea around me like a protective blanket. *I could feel like I'm enough with this woman's approval on my side.* But like anything we do in pain, it would fail.

We all carry different feelings to events like interviews and first days. You and I might show up to the same situation and experience completely different feelings because of our different stories. For me, my personal worth and performance felt like one in the same. A lack of approval would be a threat to my value. My deep need to impress this woman was driven by my feelings of insignificance or being ordinary. A flawless performance was my shield against my constant fear of being average.

I left for the therapist's house egregiously early, accounting for any potential disaster that might hinder me on the ten-minute commute. On the way, I stopped at the only florist I could find in town, where I traded what felt like most of my savings account for a modest bouquet of flowers. The positive first impression would be worth it.

Not surprisingly, I arrived approximately forty-five minutes early. Like an amateur burglar, I parked inconspicuously down the street in front of a stately gated home, turning the car on and off and lifting my butt in the air to avoid sticking to the leather seats in the thick August heat. When 11:00 a.m. finally came, I knocked on the bright red door of the woman's enormous white colonial-style home, clutching my fragrant savings account with a tight fist of eagerness and silently rehearsing answers to the questions I anticipated she would ask me.

After a few heart-pounding seconds, the door flung open and the woman ushered me into her sitting room. She spoke in short, rapid sentences as she whirled around the kitchen, pulling mugs and small china plates from her cabinets, pausing just long enough to abruptly ask me how I took my coffee. I didn't really have an interest in coffee at the moment, but I answered anyway, not wanting to risk acceptance by declining her beverage of choice.

"Black," I said, because it seemed like the easiest answer—a choice that was much bolder than I felt in that moment.

I glanced around the opulently decorated room. Everything

looked expensive and fragile. Long silk curtains draped and pooled luxuriously on the ornate rug. Collections of intricately painted vases were arranged neatly on the mantel. And large, framed photos of an African safari told the story of a well-traveled life.

Once refreshments were set out and pleasantries were exchanged, we settled into the cushions of her sitting room couch. Settling into conversation proved to be more difficult. I felt more like a witness on the stand than a guest. I continued to take sips of my bitter, black coffee, despite the fact that it made me want to gag, just to buy more time to form responses to her rapid-fire questions.

"What credentials and certifications do you have?"

"Why did you become a therapist when you were so young?"

I did my best to formulate answers that would satisfy her. But as I searched her face for some affirmation or connection, I was met with pursed lips and raised eyebrows, signaling my failure to prove myself worthy of a job and maybe even of sitting in her company. I knew my end of the conversation was falling flat. But nothing could have prepared me for the blow I received when she interrupted me with, "I mean, all people are going to see when they look at you is a little girl who isn't worth listening to."

I have no idea how much time passed in the moment of silence that followed. I willed tears back as shame washed over me. I could feel my lips curl into a smile, but I felt certain my eyes weren't playing along. I had to remind my body to do things that it was supposed to be doing automatically, like breathing and blinking.

Her statement felt like a rock wrapped in velvet. The hurtful words were packaged with a gentle voice and a smile, but her proclamation slammed into the core of my identity. I had shared everything with her. She held my story, my experience, and my dreams, and all I could do was watch her squeeze them and shape them in ways that made me feel unworthy and exposed. Her words felt true by the power of her own say-so.

I caught a glimpse of myself in the antique gilded mirror hanging above the fireplace. I saw a little girl playing dress up, sitting on a grown-up's couch. I had a feeling this woman saw me exactly the same way. I felt powerless to do or say anything that would convince her to see me for who I was or feel differently about what she saw. I had given our conversation my very best, and it was not enough. My hopes vanished.

Certainly I felt disappointed that she did not offer me a job. Of course being rejected this time made me fearful that this was the first of many rejections to come. But her words touched a deeper fear—a wound, really. At my core I was afraid I was inadequate for the call I felt God placing on my life.

Apart from being female in a female-dominated field, there was nothing about me that fit the picture of a "New England therapist" that most people held in their minds. My observations led me to believe that counseling was commonly pursued as a second career, whereas marriage and family therapy was a vocation I felt called to immediately after completing my education. I lacked life experience that naturally comes with age. I was naive to the greater New York metropolitan-area culture, while most of the therapists I encountered were native to the area. And there was absolutely nothing I could do to change these facts. I felt that having all the right credentials and experience, the perfect image, and the admiration of others would give me the confidence that this call made sense for my life. Instead, I realized I had no hard evidence to support my claim that God had called me to be a counselor. I began to doubt that God wanted me to be a therapist at all.

Sure, I was tenderhearted and compassionate. People had called me wise my whole life, and they didn't call me "old-soul Nicole" for nothing. But could God's call be enough for my shortcomings?

I also felt unsettled by the fact that I had barely known this woman an hour and it felt like she had the power to measure my worth. The problem with performing for our significance is that we place a tremendous amount of stock in the opinions of others. We depend on outside affirmation to answer our feelings regardless of whether the people we seek it from are trusted voices in our lives. This woman's opinion mattered a great deal to me, even to the extent that my whole identity seemed to hinge on her approval. Because I thought of her as a "somebody," her lack of approval made me feel like a nobody.

Somehow I managed to politely end the conversation, get up off the woman's couch, and find my way back to the red door. She thanked me for the flowers, and before I could reply, I heard the door click behind me. Why did I feel as though a part of me were still stuck inside?

A thunderstorm had rolled in during our conversation, and it was now pouring rain. I found this to be strangely comforting—the perfect backdrop for my misery. Accepting this new definition of myself as true, I made my way back to our carriage house, feeling small and rejected.

The problem with medicating our pain with performance is that we are only as valuable as our last accomplishment. In my experience, performing well might feel good in the moment, but part of you will live in fear that you will fall off the pedestal.

Even a job well done cannot bring peace, because it simply creates another opportunity to prove that you can do it again. Like anything we do in reaction to our pain, performance leads us back to the very feelings we were trying to avoid in the first place. On the other hand, if we fail to please, our worst fears are confirmed. In this case, if you are like me, you will likely decide that you are indeed insignificant and ordinary.

When I feel this way, I often find myself chasing down friends for another opinion until I find one that satisfies my longing to be good enough. On the drive home, I called my friend Lesley, a fellow therapist back in California. Although I did not recognize it at the time, the woman's words had emptied my identity, and I was now making Lesley responsible for filling me up again. Lesley answered the phone, and I wasted no time pouring out the whole story, along with my feelings.

Lesley listened. And then her gentle voice interrupted my anxiety and shame.

"Nicole, when you're called, you're called."

There was a pause. A part of me was waiting (and hoping) for more encouragement. *That's it?! I'm called to be a therapist?! Anybody can be called. I want to be awesome!*

Though her words were nice and true and should have been a comfort, they were not exactly the words I was hoping to hear. Honestly, I wished she would tell me why that woman was so wrong and why I was so right. I wanted to be reminded of my natural ability and to know that I was the right woman for the job—the *perfect* therapist. But all Lesley said was, "Nicole, when you're called, you're called."

Admittedly, I was disappointed by Lesley's response. I had been crushed by one person's lack of approval and had bought the myth that my feelings of worthlessness could be solved with kinder words from someone else. I could have told a client or a friend that no amount of affirmation from the outside can heal the wounds we carry on the inside. Gold stars can never fill the black holes of pain. I've known this as long as I've known anything. But the absence of accolades was forcing me to acknowledge the ways in which I was dependent on others' opinions, despite what I knew to be true intellectually.

I had a lot of time to think over the next few days—more time than I preferred. I kept replaying Lesley's words in my mind. And I began to hear them differently. I was experiencing in real time what I knew to be true: the answer to the disapproval of one human being is not the approval of another. It was somewhere else entirely.

What if we don't need someone's permission to run on God's mission?

This thought was interesting to me and held the possibility of bringing me some relief.

"When you're called, you're called."

I HAD HEARD ABOUT THE IDEA of calling so often that I had lost the meaning of it in my own life. I had forgotten that calling is less about our abilities and more about our willingness to believe that God will show up in us and through us. The courage to pursue a calling is less about feeling capable and more about trusting He is able.

At the heart of my desire to work as a therapist was a longing to be used by God in a powerful way. And I wanted to feel confident that my particular set of gifts would allow me to do that well. I wanted to make sense. But in the job interview I had felt like a very small David to an overwhelming Goliath.

When David was called to be king, he was a shepherd boy and the last person to be picked out of a lineup. Like any other "last pick," he lacked all the obvious qualifications for the task God had for him. He made no sense. But God was very clear, saying, "Humans do not see what the LORD sees, for humans see what is visible, but the LORD sees the heart" (1 Samuel 16:7).

We are misguided when we focus on image, talents, and personal strengths. David's small physique is mentioned again when he is called to fight a giant. The story of David fighting Goliath has always been a Sunday school favorite and as familiar to me as the scar on my left arm. But the element of this story that stands out to me is the preparation for this battle. David's lack of stature and strength concerned King Saul. Through the lens of human understanding, David simply wasn't good enough to fight Goliath. Saul's solution to David's inadequacy was to try to protect him with more armor. Saul was hoping to compensate for David's weakness by adding more strength. The king's armor was extravagant and made to protect, but it only weighed David down (1 Samuel 17:38–40).

The same is true for all the ways we try to add strength (armor) to our weakness as a means of protection. My own armor looked like pleasing and impressing others. Your armor might have a different shape and look more like anger, criticizing yourself, or escaping reality. But like Saul's armor, these strategies will only weigh us down. They merely give the illusion of strength, but true empowerment comes from an entirely different source.

David's wisdom led him to that source. "The LORD . . . will rescue me," he said (1 Samuel 17:37).

He knew his weakness was merely an avenue of God's strength.

We can try to protect ourselves by winning people over, over-preparing, or trying to control every detail. That may work for a time, but our own protection will never be the hope that saves us. Whether it is fear, a big opportunity, another person's opinion, or something else entirely, the power of the giants we face fades in the presence of the God within us.

The weakness we experience in these moments when we feel intimidated or inadequate is not only an opportunity to depend on God's strength but also to display God's power. Paul's second letter to the Corinthians proclaims that God's grace is enough for us, and instead of feeling shame about our weaknesses we can boast about them so Christ's power may comfort us and His glory may be displayed (2 Corinthians 12:9).

Yet it is in these times that it is so easy to believe that the salve for this wound is affirmation, convincing us of our natural abilities. But this is what I now know: our own natural ability is no match for God's supernatural power moving through our weakness, including the ways in which we make no sense.

Rather than my life bearing evidence of my own talents, I needed to consider what it meant for my life to bear testimony to God's power. Certainly, experiencing the acceptance of another human being or group makes us feel safe and loved in the moment. However, even here, our confidence to walk forward toward God's calling on our lives can still be propelled by human approval—an insufficient power source.

God's call is always accompanied by His promises that we find repeated throughout Scripture. In Exodus 17 God told Moses that He was going to stand in front of Moses on the rock of

Horeb so that when Moses struck the rock, it would bring water to His people (vv. 1–7). Throughout the Old Testament, God conquered nations, giving the Israelites victory before the battle was fought. In Matthew 21, Jesus commanded His disciples to fetch Him a donkey and its foal prior to riding into Jerusalem on the day we now call Palm Sunday. Jesus told the disciples that because the Lord needed the animals, they would be handed over immediately (vv. 1–3). When God calls, He equips. When God calls, we are not alone. When God calls, He is faithful to complete that calling. When God calls, it is always for our good and for His glory.

MY CIRCUMSTANCES WOULD NOT CHANGE for quite some time. I remained unemployed for several months, and when I played the woman's words back in my mind, they still stung a little. Nonetheless, something inside me had grown from the experience. I'd remembered what it meant to be called.

Remembering this story now, I can recognize that feeling as peace. This kind of peace is our courage to move forward not because we make sense or have won the admiration and respect of others, but because God is asking us to. For one of the first times in my life, I was able to move forward with assurance because of God's call and not my own capabilities.

Perhaps I would be wise to find my rest in God's favor instead of striving to be others' favorite. Maybe we don't need someone to believe in us. Maybe we simply need to believe God.

CHAPTER 5

J. CREW AND MANNA

LOSING MY VISION

God is most glorified in us when we are most satisfied in Him.

—JOHN PIPER

That'll have to be good enough," I murmured to myself. Even with the assistance of a small, rectangular plastic board, I could never get these piles of tiny clothes to be completely straight. It was a slow night in the children's section of the J. Crew store in the quaint town of Westport. Shopping isn't usually an activity that appeals to people on a night that threatens to take its temperature below zero degrees Fahrenheit. Other employees complained of boredom, but I was grateful for the pause. Despite the small number of customers, I had managed to have quite an eventful day.

My shift started by spending almost an entire hour elbow-deep in bikini bottoms, completing one return for a woman who was traveling to the British Virgin Islands for a weekend getaway. In preparation for the trip, she had ordered online nearly every swimsuit the store carried (in multiple sizes), selected one, and then hauled the rest into the store to return. As annoyed by this tedious task as I was, I can't say I blamed her. The fluorescent lights and large mirrors in the fitting rooms seemed to conspire against you to reveal every dimple, ripple, and scar since your infant vaccinations. These were not conditions conducive to bikini shopping.

To add to the frustration, somehow nearly all of my attempts to connect with customers through friendly small talk had back-fired. There was a darling little girl who looked to be about six years old shopping with an older woman with short gray hair. I chatted with the little girl and remarked that it was the perfect day to shop with grandma.

"Grandma" looked up from her evaluation of a dress in the corner and, in a flat, no-nonsense tone, said, "I'm her mom."

Then there was the large family with five children. The mother was searching through our formal clothing options for each child. Easter was early this year, and, in an attempt to offer help, I asked if they were in search of Easter outfits. "We're Jewish," the mom said before grabbing suit pants out of my hands and turning to take care of her search on her own.

I wish my mistakes had stopped there, but shortly after the large family made their way out of the store, I asked about the due date of an obviously pregnant woman, who as it turned out had her baby eight months prior. This kind of conversation is difficult to recover from, so I just busied myself with an unnecessary task by the cash register until she was ready to check out.

With an hour left of my shift, I decided that it would be best if I just stuck to folding clothes for the remainder of the day so as not to risk putting my foot in my mouth one more time. Honestly, I didn't even want to be working this job. Though Jimmy's job transition included a small pay increase, it wasn't enough to cover our bills, let alone build our savings.

I had found a job working full time at a counseling agency, but the defining characteristic of that job was that it didn't pay. I had offered to work for free because it was the fastest way to complete the post-graduate clinical hours I needed to be licensed as a marriage and family therapist in the state of Connecticut. This combination of circumstances led me to take a job as a salesperson at J. Crew to help with our expenses.

Moving from the piles of tiny graphic tees to straighten the boys' corduroy and chino section, I couldn't contain the frustration I felt about the fact that my days looked so different from what I had imagined they would at this point in my life. I felt childish admitting this to myself, but I couldn't ignore the feeling that this job looked nothing like the job I had hoped for when we moved across the country. It wasn't that I thought I was above working in retail. On the contrary, many of the salespeople I worked with had built impressive careers and were among the top-performing salespeople in the country for this company. This role was the perfect match for their gifting. But I felt discouraged that I was working a job that had no connection to my degree or the calling I felt God had placed on my life. Jimmy's job at ESPN was clear evidence of God's movement in his career and in our life together. Where was the movement in my life?

My thoughts were interrupted when I heard my name on the walkie-talkie all employees were required to wear as a means of internal communication. I was wanted in the manager's office, which was really more like a closet with a computer in the basement stock room. My heart sank. One of the customers I had offended must have complained. When the elevator doors opened to the basement, the store manager was waiting for me in the office.

"Come on in and close the door behind you, Nicole," he said with a matter-of-fact expression on his face.

Is this what getting fired feels like? I thought.

I sat down, trying to keep my knees from touching his in this tiny office, ready to face whatever he had to say.

"We're very impressed with your work here, Nicole," he said. *What?!*

"Your sales are great, and you have good relationships with customers. We'd like to promote you to the role of personal shopper."

I was stunned.

"This is an honor we don't give many people. But the managerial team feels strongly that you have what it takes, and we see a bright future for you here at J. Crew, Nicole."

Suddenly very warm, I was embarrassed to feel tears springing to my eyes. I hoped my face didn't look as red as it felt. I didn't want to appear ungrateful, but this unexpected offer was not welcome news to me. The managers might see a bright future here for me, but I didn't see a future at all! This was supposed to be a retail job to make money on the side, not my career. I'm a therapist. I wasn't supposed to be good at this!

As much as I loved the praise, the promotion felt like an affirmation in the wrong direction—that having a flourishing counseling career would remain a dream. I liked praise better on my own terms.

I had prayed for progress in my career and was expectant that God would provide. And this was the progress He gave me? What did this mean about my gifts and calling in counseling? Did I get it wrong? Was I not good enough for what I actually wanted to do with my life? What if the move really was just for Jimmy and there was nothing for me here? If this was God's provision, I didn't like it.

"Thank you. I'll have to think about it," I said matter-of-factly.

"Okay . . . you do realize that essentially the only thing that changes is that your pay will increase, right?" he said, obviously confused by my response.

"I understand, and I'd like to think about it," I said politely but firmly before taking the elevator upstairs to the safety of the tiny clothes.

Back upstairs in the children's section, I continued to fold clothes, comforted by the rhythm of the mindless task. I pressed the T-shirts flat, tucking the arms in and folding the small articles of clothing like a flimsy origami project, trying to make the tight creases stay.

What if the things I needed looked nothing like what I wanted? In California I hadn't felt that I needed rescue. But if God was calling us to Connecticut, is it possible that it was because He had something better—circumstances and opportunities that were *beyond* my own expectations and dreams?

CHAPTER 16 IN THE BOOK OF EXODUS tells the story of how God provided manna and quail for the Israelites just after their rescue from Egypt. The desert wilderness was a stark contrast to the picture of freedom they had dreamed about. I can imagine that they envisioned freedom to look like safety, where their every desire was fulfilled. If they shared my heart in this moment, I'm guessing they were hoping that freedom would come with financial security, opportunities, the comfort of routine, and the realization of their dreams on their terms.

But in the unknown, they demanded answers—and God responded to their attempts to ground themselves by giving His people the opportunity to trust Him instead. He not only met their physical needs but showed them who He was. God's instructions were simple: Every morning there would be manna on the ground, and every evening there would be quail. On the sixth day, the Israelites were to collect twice as much as they needed because they would rest on the seventh day. His question was simple: *Do you trust Me to give you exactly what you need?*

The word *manna* literally means "what is it?"—a description of the Israelites' response to what God had given them. Convinced of their own vision and plans, God's people had trouble recognizing His care for them. It was a struggle to trust God for their daily bread and take Him at His word. Some gathered extra food, and it spoiled. They didn't trust God to move when they were still. Others failed to gather enough on the sixth day, taking for granted that it would be there on the seventh day despite what the Lord had told them. It was difficult to have faith that His provision was not only enough but exactly what they needed. They didn't recognize the miracle.

REACHING FOR ANOTHER STACK of T-shirts, I wondered if I was at risk of missing the miracle too. Was I so focused on my own moves that I was missing the opportunity to marvel at God's movement in my life? Was I so worried about the outcome of my own plans that I was missing the wonder of watching His purpose unfold? Was I so committed to my own vision that I was failing to recognize God's provision?

I reflected on the months I had spent here. I remembered the tears and feelings of dread each day when Jimmy dropped me off for my shift. But just beyond my reluctant heart, I remembered the thrill of laughing with some of my coworkers, piercing the loneliness I felt from knowing no one else in Connecticut during those first few months. I could see the conversations with my fellow employees that somehow led to curiosity about my faith. I could see the look on a customer's face when I remembered her name from the week before. I recalled the many sweet conversations I had with Jimmy in the car on the way to and from my shifts. *Manna*. God had provided just what I needed. I just didn't recognize it.

PICTURE YOUR LIFE FOR A MOMENT. Are there areas of your present story that feel as though they serve no purpose? Do you stare into your days and wonder what's in it for you? Perhaps, like me, you have a job that pays the bills, but you have to squint to see your gifts and talents among the piles of what seems to you like busywork. Maybe you work inside the home and clock hours scrubbing crusty Cheerios off the countertops and googling how to erase crayon marks off the painted walls, and your calling seems to have been lost in the laundry.

Or possibly this season has been defined by waiting for the fulfillment of a dream, which might make these days feel like a waste of time. Take another minute to look at these more confusing and mundane elements of your life. Walk around them and take notice of what they look like from different angles and perspectives. What character has been strengthened in you because of those circumstances? What gifts did you discover about yourself that you might not have otherwise? Are there any moments when you can recognize what God had been up to in the midst of your disappointment? I am learning that sometimes there is treasure to find in the wake of a vision that's been lost.

Many times we struggle to recognize the manna in our hands, to trust that God remembers us and is with us. It's as if Jesus is walking shoulder to shoulder with us, but we don't recognize Him in our midst. Consider the disciples who were walking on Emmaus road and how confused they must have been in the days that followed Jesus' death. The cross must have looked nothing like the victorious ending that they had in mind. Their hope had led them to loss. The future they dreamed about was not their reality. And when two of them found themselves debriefing the horrifying events of the past couple of days, Jesus—their resurrected Lord—joined them on the path and in their conversation. Hope was walking with them, but the disciples couldn't recognize Him because the appearance of their Lord did not match their expectation.

THE JOB AT J. CREW looked nothing like my own plans for the future. Nothing about it felt like a fit for my gifting or my dreams. This was not a road I wished to walk. I would prefer to quit than take this promotion. But in the chaos of the unknown and the unmet expectations, would I be so committed to my own vision that I would miss the miracle of my Hope walking with me?

Maybe Jesus really had been walking right beside me. Somehow, in this unwanted season, we had a church that was beginning to feel like a family. Jimmy was thriving at ESPN and loving the people he worked with. Our community of friends was expanding, and the relationships inside it were deepening. I was working as a counselor and loving my work, even though it came with no pay. I had found this job at J. Crew quickly, allowing us to make ends meet. And even among the piles of cashmere sweaters and bauble necklaces and children's T-shirts, I could now recognize places where God had given me Himself in circumstances I did not choose for myself.

After I'd finished my work and wrapped up the closing clean-up duties, I gathered my belongings to leave. My manager opened the door for me, and I was halfway down the walkway before I turned around and said, "I'll take the job." He looked surprised, and I was a little surprised by those words myself.

Sometimes when we are waiting for what we want, we find what we need.

CALLED OUT DISCUSSION QUESTIONS

1. Think about the events and relationships in your story. What messages have you received about your significance and security?
2. What feelings did these messages leave you with?
3. Where do you see these feelings in your life today?
4. Describe a time when you experienced loss or discomfort that, looking back, ultimately led to healing, growth, or a new understanding of God.
5. What are some of the treasures that can divide your heart and cause you to become anxious?
6. How does knowing that you've been pursued by God change the way you might interact in your current and future relationships?
7. Describe a time when you felt weak or ill-equipped and how you saw God move through that weakness.
8. What are some gifts in your life that you have failed to recognize as manna (God's provision) because you were expecting the provision to look different?

PART 2

BREAKING DOWN

THE FAILURE OF BEHAVIORS THAT WERE NEVER MEANT TO WORK

CHAPTER 6

YOGIS

THE FAILURE OF CONTROL

> *Listen, are you breathing just a little, and calling*
> *it a life?*
>
> —MARY OLIVER

I am not a yogi. I generally lack the patience required for long periods of silence, deep breaths, and prolonged stretches, and I have no idea what phrases like "feel your breath" actually mean. When it comes to exercise, I prefer a good cardio sweat. But after years of migraine headaches and an ever-growing pile of emergency room bills, I was feeling defeated.

I had tried everything else, from prescription medications, massage, and acupuncture, to strange home remedies that included unusual herbs and odd combinations of heat and ice. I had even restricted my diet by eliminating gluten, dairy, and soy, to the envy of no one. And though these strategies helped, they didn't heal. I decided to give in to my friends' repeated nudges and give yoga a try.

When I bought my first yoga mat at the local athletic store, the saleswoman handed me my purchase with the pride of a first-time mom watching her child learn to walk—as if I had found the answer to all of my woes in this piece of long, flat, purple rubber.

Still skeptical, I arrived at my first class and selected a space in the back left corner of the dimly lit room, so I could be as close to invisible as possible. I had never liked doing things I had not yet mastered, and it felt best to keep my incompetence hidden from as many people as I could.

The instructor walked in looking as if he had just gotten off a plane from Bali. He was barefoot and wore loose parachute pants and a tight tank top. A skinny, long beard trailed off his chin like a trickling waterfall, offsetting the short, Pebbles Flintstone–like ponytail on the top of his otherwise bald head. I had never seen such a creature in our buttoned-up town. I wasn't even aware this species existed in Fairfield County.

A few minutes into the class I was "feeling my breath" and losing my patience.

Where is this going?

What will this do for me?

I don't think it's working . . .

I was already annoyed that this felt more like relaxation than exercise. *What is the point?*

As if reading the transcript of my thoughts, the instructor's gentle yet direct voice answered me. "Sometimes the process is the point."

Well, all right then.

Glancing around to be sure my uncomfortable, pretzel-like pose somewhat resembled what I was supposed to be doing, I found myself tempted to compare myself to the yogis in the room. I compared my skills, or lack thereof, to those of the limber, coordinated people packed into the studio. And I compared my body to the other women who had clearly been doing this for years.

As if detecting my darting eyes, Barefoot Man said, "Don't you dare compare yourself to others . . ." His voice trailed off into the silence of the room.

Noted.

We moved to a stretch in which the goal was to reach our fingertips forward as far as we could, and it was clear we were all looking for the bottom line. *How far do we need to stretch? What do we need to do to check the box or get the gold star? When is it good enough?*

Our wandering eyes gave us away. Sensing our questions, Barefoot Man said, "When should you stop? Your body will tell you; your mind will not."

As we transitioned (some of us more smoothly than others) to the next pose, the instructor's statement stayed with me.

Your body will tell you; your mind will not.

I thought about my migraines—the reason I'd come to this class in the first place. Debilitating headaches were my body's rude way of telling me to stop. They drew lines around my capacity that I absolutely could not cross without consequences. Chronic headaches limited my schedule, forcing me to be mindful of how many hours can be booked in a day without my body quitting and forcing me to go home early. Even the types of activities I could do were limited by what my head could handle.

But I preferred not to listen. Perhaps just as painful as the migraine was the truth that there are many other elements of my life that I cannot control, such as others' opinions of me and how much I am able to accomplish in a given period of time. Headaches served as a perpetual reminder of my humanity and the harsh reality of what I am actually empowered to do, and what I would like to control but can't.

HEADACHES AREN'T THE ONLY WAY our bodies signal us to stop. Your body might toss up a different flare. You might notice other physical symptoms, such as extreme fatigue or muscle tension. You might notice a feeling of burnout, possibly with a blue cloud of depression or sadness you can't shake. Maybe you notice yourself getting irritable and short with others. Or you let resentment build in your relationships, maintaining the belief that you can do it all and be it all for everyone all the time—until you can't.

When the mind pushes past our physical or emotional limitations, we will know it. The question is, what voice will we choose to listen to? The voice that tells us that we must keep pushing for peace and joy? Or the voice that encourages us to work from the assurance of peace and joy?

I loathe a day wiped clean of appointments and plans for the sake of sitting and struggling in pain. One would think that the headache is the worst part of that scenario, but the lack of control feels worse to me than the pain itself. Being limited in my ability to please others, meet my own expectations, and execute my own plans is an aspect of my humanity I prefer to ignore. Also, I don't want to believe that my capabilities and the number of projects and commitments I might be able to handle are less than someone else's. So I keep pushing—pushing past fatigue, burnout, and physical pain in the name of proving that I am as capable as I want to be.

Remember, we all adopt reactive tendencies and habits to protect ourselves from the pain we carry about our value and our sense of safety. These behaviors tend to be short-term solutions that create longer-term problems. In other words, what feels like a quick fix in the moment almost always reinforces the pain. Some of us blame: we get angry and assign responsibility to everyone but ourselves. Some of us numb by escaping into other worlds, such as the lives of characters on a screen or awe-inspiring Instagram accounts. Others control, even in areas that are not theirs to take over. And still others might mercilessly shame themselves. These are just a few examples of the many ways that we can attempt to medicate our wounds.

These reactions to our pain are not pleasant to look at. You will likely not feel proud to name them. But as the character Scout recently reminded me in Aaron Sorkin's Broadway adaptation of Harper Lee's *To Kill a Mockingbird*, "Things you can't see are a lot scarier than the things you can."[1] They lose their power when they are exposed to light. Naming the heart of the heartache is the beginning of healing.

When it comes to trying to protect myself from pain, control has long been my go-to and personal favorite. For as long as I can remember, I've used hard work as a drug against my feelings of inadequacy, believing the lie that my own efforts and grit were enough to make me feel secure. Pushing past my own limitations was just one of the ways that I used control to avoid the pain of feeling powerless against my circumstances.

There are many faces of control. The control in your life might show up differently than mine. Sometimes control looks like making countless lists for ourselves and loved ones. Other times it looks like taking over a project, trusting no one's gifting or ideas but our own. Or it might show up as anxiety—feeling out of control when events don't go exactly as planned. But whatever costume it wears, control leaves no room for the valuable input of others. Control cuts us off from learning from each other and being enriched by others' ideas and approaches to a problem or project. With control, we never get to experience the intimacy that comes from vulnerability and trusting someone other than ourselves.

It's worth noting that I used to be secretly proud of my own reactive tendencies. If we all have them, I was glad to be someone who shames and controls with performance and becoming overly responsible, because it seemed to me that these protective strategies were less harmful than others. But the hard truth is that *anything* we do in reaction to our pain is relationally destructive and profoundly unhelpful in facilitating meaning and connection.

THE YOGA CLASS HAD PROGRESSED, but I was just sitting in the back corner in a slouchy crisscross-applesauce position, reflecting. I was not a stranger to physical limitations. As a young ballet dancer, I lacked the flexibility and coordination and just about everything else I needed to excel. As a swimmer, my shoulders were about half the width necessary to be great in the water, and flip turns were my ever-present Achilles' heel. As a runner, I was long and lean, but I was no gazelle.

Graduate school was the worst season in terms of intensity and frequency of headaches. I don't think I studied a single day of my first quarter without a migraine. But resting did not feel like an option. Up until now, my strategy for coping with my limitations had been to pretend that these lines my body had drawn did not exist and to outwork everybody else. My mind was driven by my ambition, the goals I would like to accomplish, what I would *like* to be able to do, or worse, what I felt I *should* be able to do. My mind held the expectations, the dreams, and the determination. Certainly the mind is important and good, but it had become the only voice that mattered in my life and the archenemy of my body.

There are many triggers for my migraines, but the headaches and the emergency room visits I'd been experiencing in this latest season were a direct result of my panicked hustle—a clear sign that overworking and performing were not helpful to me at all. I had turned down the volume on my emotional and physical needs, operating from the belief that the higher my capacity, the higher my value. Acknowledging my limitations would have meant that I was defective in some way. I lived as though my life were a product of my efforts alone and believed that if I worked hard enough, I could make my life look like the life I wanted—I could control my way to a safe place. I felt time was only worth something if you have something to show for it. Though I probably would not have said that this was the case, it was at the core of all my choices and actions.

Our move and my change in circumstances was accompanied by a slower pace than I preferred to keep. When people would ask me out to lunch or coffee, they naturally asked, "What day and time is good for you?" And I would half-jokingly answer, "Any day, any time, my friend" as I tried to squish the shame I felt in being so available. This move created wider margins in my life than I was used to, and I was compulsively creative in finding ways to fill the empty space. Intellectually, I knew this was a season, not my new forever normal. I also (correctly) predicted that there would come a time when I would long for this season—that the empty space would feel like a welcome break instead of a mark of shame. But this was not that time.

I was preoccupied with the longing for all the things that were not filling the white space as quickly as I wanted. Would I get a job? Would I build a full practice? Would I have to work in retail forever because I might not actually have what it takes to be a therapist in this part of the country? What if there really wasn't anything here for me? I defined myself by how I spent my time. This made the thought of surrendering to rest a scary one.

Still sitting in the back of the dark yoga studio, I had given up on the class and was completely ignoring the instructor's prompts. He didn't seem to mind. That's the wonderful thing about yoga. There's a "you do you" mentality, and it was working for me in this moment. It was a small victory, but for perhaps one of the first times in my life, I was feeling free to let go and rest simply because it was what I needed.

On the traffic-clogged drive home, I continued to think about the purpose of rest—not just taking a nap or a break, but finding security in the midst of unmet expectations and tasks left undone—soul rest. I reflected on the fact that rest was a part of God's own nature, and a rhythm of work and rest was His intentional design for creation—a template formed in the very beginning for how to live. God Himself does not need rest, but He chose it for Himself in the creation of the earth. And He must have felt strongly that it was important for us as well if resting on the Sabbath was included in the Ten Commandments.

I realized that part of me viewed this structure of work and rest as stifling. Structure and freedom felt mutually exclusive. But I was starting to recognize that physical limitations and His command to rest—like all of God's laws—are avenues that lead to life, where we find more depth, beauty, celebration, and intimacy with Him.

As I walked through the door of our tiny bungalow and put my yoga mat away, I decided to do some more digging on rest. I was still skeptical that yoga was for me, but I knew that pushing beyond my limits out of fear of what would happen, or who I would be if I stopped, was not working for me anymore. I searched through my concordance, looking for all the verses I could find on rest. As I studied them, I came across a verse in Isaiah that seemed to answer my internal questions.

> For the Lord GOD, the Holy One of Israel, has said:
> "You will be delivered by returning and resting;
> your strength will lie in quiet confidence.
> But you are not willing." (30:15)

The "quiet confidence" was at the heart of the rest I most needed in my life. Yes, the courage to stop attempting to be in control of everything or to simply take a break would be a step—a significant one for me. But to do so, knowing that I am empowered to do some things but I cannot and do not have to control it all, is the rest my heart most craved. I realized that my strength and confidence had mostly been in my own efforts. I had been living like my own work was going to earn me the peace I longed for.

TO MANY OF US IT FEELS LIKE PEACE and joy can only be found on the other side of hard work. Like the Israelites who gathered extra manna, this "quiet confidence" can seem foreign outside of our own efforts. We are afraid to leave things undone and outside of our control. Rest is something to be earned—a reward for a job well done.

But the truth is that the Sabbath never starts when the work is done. It starts when it starts, inviting us to a different kind of rest—a quiet confidence—a trusting rest that assures that the gifts in this life are a result of God's grace, not our own grit.

Both work and rest are important—even sacred. One only makes sense in relationship to the other. In the rhythm of the two, we find freedom. Every time we ignore our humanity and let our desire for control pull us out of God's design for work and rest, we rob ourselves of experiencing His grace—the grace that says we are loved because we are created, not because of the life we are creating.

The breaking down of our control reveals the enduring strength in surrendering to God. It's not as if we can control nothing. The answer to our need to do it all and be it all is not to give up or take no responsibility. Surrender is simply an acknowledgement that we are empowered to do some things, but our lives are ultimately shaped by God's will, not our own.

More than an excuse or an escape, surrendering our control is an encounter with Jesus. Confronting our limitations might be the very place where we seek God's strength instead of relying on our own. Here we will find security outside of our own control. We can participate in the celebration of Christ, remembering what His death and resurrection means for our human condition: that we are safe and loved not because of what we do or what is in our control but because of what Christ has already done. Here, we find that our limitations can actually serve as a vehicle of freedom in our lives—freedom that can only come from Christ.

I am still not a yogi. Honestly, I'm not sure I ever will be. But I am learning to listen to my body and give it a stronger voice in my decision-making. I'm training my brain to see my physical fragility as an opportunity to rely on strength outside myself and find relief in the fact that my life isn't fashioned by my own efforts. And when I struggle to find this truth, I often find my way back to my yoga mat. I plant my feet firmly on the purple rubber and breathe in and out. Sometimes the process is the point.

CHAPTER 7

GLUTEN-FREE PASTA

THE FAILURE OF PERFECTION

> *We cultivate love when we allow our most*
> *vulnerable and powerful selves to be deeply seen*
> *and known, and when we honor the spiritual*
> *connection that grows from that offering with*
> *trust, respect, kindness, and affection.*
> —BRENÉ BROWN

The congested traffic curved for miles ahead of me, looking like a winding line of red ants marching down I-95. Tiny droplets of summer rain dotted my windshield as the smell of wet pavement wafted through my open window. I glanced at the glowing clock on my dashboard, hoping I wouldn't be late to meet my friend Jeannie for dinner.

Jeannie was a new friend but someone I had admired and looked up to since I moved to Connecticut just more than a year prior. She was one of the very first people I met at church, and I was drawn to her magnetic personality and her uncanny ability to make me feel known and understood when I talked to her. I appreciated her candor and her infectious sense of humor. I just liked being around her. I knew Jeannie loved me for exactly who I was. But my admiration for her was accompanied by a strong desire for her to like me too. I had been here before with other friends I held in high esteem. No matter how safe and loving a friend had proven themselves to be, I fought the urge to edit myself and present an image I imagined this friend would like.

I was grateful to find a parking spot quickly and rushed toward the Italian restaurant we had agreed on, cutting through the humidity of the late August evening. I found Jeannie at a table situated in the corner of the patio strung with bistro lights. She had a glass of pinot noir waiting for me. God bless her! We had chosen this particular Italian restaurant because of its relatively vast selection of gluten-free pasta dishes. Carbohydrates of this nature are a true treat for the gluten-intolerant, and it was rare to actually have choices.

After we caught up on the recent details of our lives, our pasta dishes (with extra marinara sauce) arrived. We continued the conversation while eating, and I asked Jeannie about what her life looked like before she had kids.

She paused. The look on her face let me know I had stumbled upon something painful. Her eyes turned down and to the right before looking straight into mine as she replied, "Have I told you

I was married before?" She hadn't. But I could tell this question unlocked memories of a season that hurt my friend deeply.

Jeannie proceeded to share a piece of her history that I hadn't known—a tale of a life that took place long before the life she lives and loves now. She detailed an unhealthy relationship characterized by heartache that was no fault of her own. Ultimately, she made the brave but devastating decision to walk away from a marriage that could not be restored. As she introduced me to this chapter of her story, sharing the events that led her to here and now, I quietly swept tears from my face. I found myself wishing I could step into those events she described and become a character who could take away even just a little of the pain she must have felt.

When Jeannie had told me everything she had to share, she looked up at me with a vulnerable expression.

I have never asked Jeannie how she felt after telling me her story. But I know how I feel when I share from the more vulnerable places of my heart. I start wondering if people will stay. My fear is not so much that they will physically get up and leave. I worry that revealing pieces of my true inner self, or the parts of myself that might not appeal to people, will cause others to love me less or, at the very least, view and value me differently. My worries usually take the form of questions like *Does this information change the way they think of me? Do I still hold the same place in their minds and hearts? Did I expose myself and give away too much? Am I just as special to them as I was before they knew this about me?*

Typically, I have avoided putting myself in a position of hearing the answers to these questions by trying to be as perfect as possible, fearing rejection. Despite having close friendships growing up, in which vulnerability was comfortable and commonplace, I had difficulty trusting that I would appeal to others if I wasn't perfect. I imagined instant dismissal if I failed to meet all of a person's needs and expectations. I was keenly aware that I was not perfect. But between rejection and perfection, perfection was the preferred option.

Jeannie showed me another way—an entirely new path, free from the limiting (and exhausting) choices of rejection or perfection that I had typically given myself. I was honored that she would share her heart with me. But more than the events themselves, I was struck by how I felt toward her. I had always liked Jeannie and admired so many of her qualities. Now, I not only liked her but was stunned by the level of love I felt for her. Her willingness to share with raw vulnerability didn't cause me to back up but to lean in. I had no interest in walking away. I wanted to walk alongside her. I felt close to her and honored to hold this painful part of her journey with her. It was a joy to be entrusted with both her past and the feelings that remain.

No words felt sufficient to communicate what I deeply wanted her to know. I found myself wishing I could rewind time and rescue her from all of it. I wanted to take any lingering feelings she carried as a result of these painful events and kill those lies with truth. I wanted to squeeze her tight enough to make her never forget how loved and worthy she is. But with these not being viable options, I reached under the table to find her hand. I held it tight and, through my tears, managed to speak the words, "I love you, and I am honored to know and hold your story."

Jeannie's willingness to entrust her heart to me shaped my own heart. I could feel a meaningful shift then, but I didn't realize the level to which that dinner would serve as a marker for me to return to again and again. Jeannie opened a door that our culture generally tells us to keep closed, and the experience of walking through it was transformational for me. Her vulnerability caused the space between us to collapse, and it challenged my ideas about what really draws us to one another.

I had always operated from the belief that the more perfect I was, the more loved I could be and the more secure my position was inside that love. My strategy for getting close to people looked more like winning them over than connecting with them. But performance is not intimacy. Applause is not love. Perfection doesn't hold the key to connection.

I used to wonder about the harm in relying on perfection to cope with my fears of rejection. How could my perfectionism be hurtful to others? Wasn't everyone grateful for my high standards? But the gentle and kind feedback I've received over the years from Jimmy and close friends is that when I maintain impossible standards for myself, it's very difficult for others to imagine that I don't carry those same impossible standards for them.

The amount of grace I show myself when I am not perfect (exactly zero) is the amount of grace they experience from me. In my need to feel safe from rejection, I became an unsafe person to share with. When I choose to hide behind perfectionist tendencies, others don't feel permission to fully be themselves or free to make mistakes around me. It's difficult for them to experience love from me that is not attached to their performance.

Perfect is shiny and sterile and might be nice to look at—for awhile. But perfect doesn't move you. It doesn't challenge you to think differently or compel you to feel anything that draws you close. Vulnerability is messy, yes. But it is present, and raw, and moves us to experience joy outside of ourselves. My evening with Jeannie demonstrated beautifully how our vulnerabilities, not our capabilities, draw us close to one another.

EVER SINCE ADAM AND EVE ate from the Tree of Knowledge of Good and Evil, recognized their nakedness, and felt shame, the human race (regardless of culture) has been prone to hiding. We have become people who are tempted to shield our private selves with carefully constructed public selves. Adam and Eve physically hid themselves with fig leaves. We don't tend to use foliage in this way anymore, but we are a people familiar with hiding, aren't we? And hiding doesn't just look like withdrawal. Hiding is anything we do to try to protect ourselves from pain: blame, shame, control, or escape.

As humans we're confused by this notion of vulnerability. This struggle is not new. It appears that people in Jesus' time were confused as well. We see this lack of understanding on the part of the people Jesus related with during His ministry here on earth. His interactions held something important in common, woven like a golden thread through the Gospels. Every relationship and each encounter played a role in telling the bigger story that the only thing we need to be close to Jesus is . . . nothing.

I recognize myself in the disciples' confusion when they asked Jesus who among them was the greatest. They assumed that the better and stronger they became, the closer to God's favor they would be. But again and again, Jesus gently countered people's ideas about greatness by seeking after the lost, making an invitation to the outcast, and healing the desperate and helpless. Jesus told us to be childlike in our faith. He wasn't encouraging us to be immature but dependent—to be in a position of recognizing our imperfection and need for Him instead of being self-sufficiently perfect.

Perhaps Jesus' relationships here on earth have something to teach us about our relationships with each other. Intimacy is not the fruit of being perfect but of being people who acknowledge our need for Christ. This is where transformation begins. The connection we were made to crave comes from telling the truth about where we've been, where we are, and where we are going, not simply talking about our self-achieved perfect arrival.

For me, this often looks like sharing the ways in which God has transformed me and is challenging me to grow in my journey. Vulnerability puts God's glory on display instead of our own. A willingness to share our whole stories allows us to see more of God's story—even if we don't fully understand it yet.

Where do we begin? We start somewhere, right now. We start opening the door to let others in to where we've been and where we are and the places we'd like to go in our areas of growth. We give ourselves grace for the areas we're working on or that we wish were different, knowing that the amount of grace we give ourselves is the measure of grace we will have to offer others. And we recognize that vulnerability and boundaries are not mutually exclusive. We share different things in different ways with different people depending on the safety that's been built in that relationship. This won't go perfectly either. Sometimes we'll share too much. Sometimes we'll hold back. But we learn and we continue to find the courage to show up and share vulnerably, not *for* our significance but *from* it.

Vulnerability has been a primary topic of conversation in American culture in recent years. But I can't help but feel that it is a concept that can be easily misused. As I considered my ideas about vulnerability, I recognized it to be a strength that has great power and therefore must be used properly. It felt important that I steward this neediness well, which meant taking it to the right Person. Yes, God built us for relationship and designed us to be in interdependent community with one another. But being interdependent and dependent are different. God is the only safe place for our dependence to land because He is the only one who can fulfill. What are we looking for when we decide to be open with others? Are we hoping to get something from someone else that only God can give, like validation and affirmation? Are we looking *for* our value or are we sharing *from* it?

THE NIGHT WAS TURNING COLDER, and the dishes were long ago scraped clean. Jeannie's friendship had shown me how healthy vulnerability is a willingness to be seen and share deeply, knowing that our significance is protected from the outcome or reaction we receive from others. I wanted less hiding and more of her courage and more of this connection I felt between the two of us.

For the first time all evening, I realized just how aware the other restaurant patrons were of us. We were quite a sight: two blubbering blondes gripping hands over gluten-free pasta. We said our goodbyes by toasting with our empty wine glasses to the imperfect and the gift of leaving this night with a different and deeper friendship.

CHAPTER 8

WAVES OF GRACE

THE FAILURE OF PERFORMANCE

*You are the most loved not when you're pretending
to have it all together; you are actually the most
loved when you feel broken and falling apart.*
—ANN VOSKAMP

I was only eight weeks along, but already so much anticipation had been building toward our first doctor's appointment, when we would see and hear our baby for the first time. I could still see the look on Jimmy's face when I surprised him on Valentine's Day with the news that I was pregnant. Neither of us could stop crying for twenty minutes, leaving the other restaurant patrons to wonder about the storyline unfolding at our table.

We purchased a beautiful leather-bound journal and began to write letters to our little one, chronicling even the earliest days of his or her story. I had dreams for this baby and had envisioned a life far into the future. With my dreams came questions. Would I have a daughter or a son? Would he or she like music and theater, or football and soccer, or both? What gifts would God store inside this child? Would the baby have Jimmy's thick hair and sweet smile or my blue crescent-shaped eyes?

And with my questions came prayers. I prayed that my baby would feel cherished and wanted. I prayed that my baby would grow up knowing how to celebrate the gifts God would give him or her. I prayed that my baby would always feel safe and secure in our home and would trust Jimmy and me with the burdens and hopes carried in his or her heart. Most of all, I prayed that this baby would know his or her identity and sense of belonging in Christ. So many plans, prayers, and wonderings had taken place on behalf of this unborn life already—even before our move to Connecticut two and a half years prior. The beginning was promising.

After a long, expectant wait in our doctor's waiting room, the nurse finally ushered us into the ultrasound room. We were so excited we hardly heard the routine instructions the ultrasound technician recited like a tape recorder. She prompted me in short, staccato phrases as I looked at the screen, trying to absorb the moment. *This is it!*

As a therapist, I am trained to read facial expressions. I learned early on that you can understand just as much, if not more, information from a person's face than you can from their words. In this case, I read the bad news before I heard it.

"I'm so sorry. There is no heartbeat."

My body reacted with sweat, tears, and shaking before my brain could comprehend the reality.

"What does this mean?" I whispered. Of course I knew what it meant, but I was grasping at hope that couldn't be found on the screen.

"It means this isn't a viable pregnancy," she said matter-of-factly.

My arms flailed, searching for Jimmy in the dark room, numb to the fact that he was already there. He pulled me closer as I sobbed. He sobbed too.

It isn't supposed to be this way . . .

"I'm right here," he said.

A MONTH LATER, THE MARINE AIR still grayed the morning as I watched my bare feet imprint the wet sand in steady rhythm. Our friends had gifted us their home in Florida for the week, and we felt grateful to be elsewhere for a while—especially since this particular "elsewhere" boasted temperatures we hadn't seen in months.

Something had begun stirring in me the night before. Thoughts tumbled around in my mind like laundry taking too long to dry. And as the night gave in to the morning light, I had remained alert. It was the middle of our vacation, but Jimmy was needed for a meeting in Los Angeles and had to leave for twenty-four hours. He'd left early that morning, leaving me to spend the day on a Naples beach by myself.

In theory, this was an opportunity for me to rest. But the pause created space, welcoming emotions I had been trying to protect myself from since our doctor's appointment just over a month ago. In the stillness and the quiet of my mind, I could feel the dam breaking—a force too strong for my willpower to contain. The pain demanded my attention like a tantruming two-year-old, and it would not be ignored.

I was still struggling to accept my new reality and the "what will never be" of it all. The story of the year 2014 and all the milestones I had dreamed of celebrating—the ones I was already eagerly anticipating and actively preparing for—vanished in a moment. But the excitement that accompanied those dreams was taking longer to fade. The beginning of this baby's story felt so special. I was confused and pained by the fact that I would not see the story continue. My family had celebrated this baby already and shifted plans to accommodate the months surrounding the due date. So much started that would never be finished. Dreams are powerful constructs in our minds and are not easily disassembled by a reality we do not wish to see.

To be quite honest, I never thought miscarriage would happen to me. I had counseled women going through the loss of a baby, and I had walked through it with many loved ones. But somehow I carried a hidden, naive belief that I could put myself in the "safe" category. I had no family history of miscarriage and had done everything right for that little one. I read all the recommended books. I ate an exorbitant amount of protein and took all the right vitamins for my baby to develop as he or she should. I rested, which was perhaps the biggest challenge of them all. I prayed faithfully. But my hard work and determination to do it all and to do it all well had not worked. My performance wasn't enough. I would not get to meet this baby in this lifetime, and I could not fix it. The fragility of life became real to me, and the miracle of life became exactly what it always was—a miracle.

Some well-intentioned friends tried to comfort me by telling me that miscarriages are normal. "This happens to so many women," they said. "It's so common," they told me. Well, nothing about miscarriage felt common to me. The "common cold" was common. How could the loss of a life and the fact that we do not get to meet one of our babies this side of heaven feel normal?

Others tried to console me by taking the long view. "Someday you'll have all of your kids and this loss will make sense. You'll love your kids so much, you won't even miss this one," they predicted. "You just need to get pregnant again and have another baby," they said—as if it was that easy. How could I think about another baby when the only baby I wanted was the one I just lost? I hoped our future held the birth of more children, but even then, how could the addition of one life negate the sting of the loss of another?

I held on to hope that this pain would not be wasted—that God would somehow use it as fertile ground for a more intimate relationship with Him, deeper connections with others, and growth inside myself. But even if I was blessed with these gifts to carry with me into the future, I'm still not sure the loss would ever make sense. Demand as we might, some pain never sees answers.

I was about a quarter of a mile down the beach when the clouds began to turn pink, previewing daybreak. All of a sudden, my heart started racing and my hands shook involuntarily. The air was cool, but I was sweating profusely, and no breath seemed to be capturing the air I needed. I was not okay, and I could not make myself okay. I sat down on the sand, hoping that being on the ground would ground me.

I could only recall feeling this way one other time. During one of my last cross-country meets in eighth grade, I rounded the final corner in the lead. A girl from another school, Emmy Lou, and I had battled for first place all season. All I had to do to win was give it one final push on the straightaway. I could see the parents cheering in the distance. My coach was running alongside me, both cheering and instructing me to the very end.

With about fifty yards left—unexpectedly and for reasons I couldn't understand—I was running at a forty-five degree angle, and my arms were making huge circles like windmills, my face barely suspended above the ground. My mind had no idea what my body was doing, and then I collapsed onto the dirt path. I could hear the pounding sneakers, including Emmy Lou's, rush by me. I vaguely remember my coaches grabbing me and pulling me to the side. Despite my will to move forward, my body had quit.

After reflecting on my day at school later that day, it was clear that I was simply so busy doing what I needed to do that I had forgotten to hydrate and properly fuel my body. Not unlike my struggle with migraines, I let my need for accomplishment and productivity dictate my choices over what my body was asking for. Now, years later, I wondered if I had failed to listen to my needs again—this time, my emotional needs. My body was quitting.

I knew the miscarriage itself wasn't physically my fault. But shame is tenacious in finding fault within. Had I not been grateful enough for this baby? Had I taken the pregnancy for granted? Were my worries about my ability to negotiate being a therapist and a mom a failure to trust God? A part of me worried that I had failed to please God, and the miscarriage and the feelings that followed were an opportunity to perform—to win Him over with my strength and maturity. I projected my pain and protective strategies onto God and His Word, creating a faulty theology.

As much as those failed attempts at comforting me felt wrong, a part of me believed them. I felt the need to be stronger than the pain. Even in the midst of what had been one of the most difficult months of my life, I chose performance as my primary method of protection against the feeling that I had failed to be good enough.

It was easy to see that I had been minimizing my feelings in the name of being strong. I explained my hurt and confusion away with statistics. I quickly turned conversations to focus on other people so as not to allow my pain to take up too much space in a dialogue or relationship. Even on the darkest days, I refrained from asking for help when I needed it, mistaking vulnerability for weakness. I wanted to handle it, and I wanted to handle it well.

Shame is often what sets the stage for performance, so it's not unusual for performance to quickly follow shame when it comes to coping with pain. In this case, shame had convinced me that this miscarriage was the result of a personal failure. I felt safer moving into the future with a good performance under my belt. If I had to endure this loss, it felt good to have the admiration of others on my side.

But as my tears gave way to sobs on the beach, I realized that my most dazzling performance had been for God. I never wanted to lose another baby, and there was a part of me that felt that if I could make God proud of me and of how I handled my pain, I would pass this test with flying colors and never have to take it again. I felt that if I could demonstrate my spiritual maturity and say all the "right" things, maybe this loss would become a nightmare of the past.

I wanted to be fixed before I approached God in prayer,

revealing my lifelong assumption that the less fragile and flawed I am, the more lovable I become. My prayers were filled with spiritual platitudes—empty words that served as pretty packaging for my raw feelings. I was terrified to tell Him how I actually felt or let Him know I was confused by His lack of intervention. I kept my prayers small, asking God for nothing, afraid of appearing needy or ungrateful for the blessings I had. I was living as if the less I needed Him, the more He would love me.

As I watched the waves curl their lips and spit fizz on the sand, I reflected on a conversation I had with my mentor, Terry, just after our loss. He had listened and offered wisdom and comfort. He prayed for me out loud over Skype from across the country. He and his wife, Sharon, had always loved me so well, and this conversation was no exception. I couldn't recall everything we talked about through my tears, but just before we hung up, he said one thing that would always stay with me: "Nicole, I know you will be a good steward of your pain."

Sitting on the beach by myself, unable to control the emotion and thinking about the truth in Terry's words, I saw how I'd tried to manage my pain with shame and performance, and it failed me. It only kept me further from the comfort I longed for and needed. Performing for God was my attempt at protection against the pain of loss, but what I really needed was to steward my pain in a way that cultivated connection with Him.

THE DETAILS OF YOUR STORY might look different from mine. Perhaps you've looked upon a tragedy in your life and, like me—against all reason and rationale—you've found a way to take responsibility for a burden you were never meant to carry. Maybe you've looked upon a mistake you've made or a destructive pattern you're ashamed of and concluded that you're too much for the grace of God to cover and your own goodness is your only hope.

Or, possibly, you feel that a stellar performance on your part is the only way you will be noticed or cared for—the only way you can make up for feeling defective or deficient. You've perfected your performance to keep from slipping through the cracks. You can make a drug out of anything, including behaviors we as human beings often celebrate, such as independence, self-achieved strength, and the applause of others. But like any drug, the effects don't last. The relief is only temporary.

Being a good steward of your pain doesn't mean wishing it away, finding a way to be blind to what is wrong in this life, or ignoring the pain of what's been lost or broken. The first step is being willing to see, feel, and speak the reality of what hurts.

Jesus said that those who mourn are blessed. Those words challenged my assumptions about what it means to be blessed. I viewed blessing as the absence of suffering. I saw myself as more special when I was the hero of the story—when my own efforts saved me from the pit of grief. I saw myself as safer when I was numb to the sting of loss. But Jesus spoke a different truth. "Those who mourn . . . will be comforted" Jesus said (Matthew 5:4), telling us the good news that grief—in all its messiness and ugliness—can be an avenue of God's grace in our lives.

Instead of being someone who is blessed with a comfortable life, I was beginning to see that a blessed person is someone who has been awakened to her hunger for Christ and is now ready to be filled by Him alone.

This kind of blessing is for you too. You can lay down whatever it is that keeps you numb to the sharp pangs of hunger. You don't have to protect yourself from the emptiness with anger, shame, distraction, or even a dazzling performance. The emptiness wasn't meant to be covered but filled.

Maybe your struggle looks like mine. You wrestle with the need to fix yourself, and you remain committed to proving yourself and earning your own way. But Jesus came to offer another way. Through His death and resurrection, we remember that our hope is not in fixing ourselves. Rather, we find hope when we focus our gaze on a Savior who fixed Himself to a cross.

Being in relationship with Jesus gives us a clearer vision. Walking this life with Him means we feel the sharp dissonance between the way things are and the way things are supposed to be, ushering us into honest grief.

In the throes of such grief, we can remember that Jesus Himself grieved too. We read about Jesus' sorrow several times in the Gospels. But the story I identified most with in that moment was the story of Lazarus's death. In what is most famously known as the shortest verse in the Bible, we read that "Jesus wept" over this loss (John 11:35). He knew the miracle that was about to come, but He still felt the fullness of His sorrow. His weeping made a statement about the reality that we live in the gap between what is and what should be. The loss, the brokenness, and the pain are not what God intended for us in His original plan. Jesus' weeping answered my attempts to minimize my pain by assuring me that no matter how prevalent painful circumstances might be, they are *not* the way things are supposed to be.

Shame and invulnerable self-sufficiency were only serving as barriers to the connection I desperately needed in order to heal.

Performance protected me from the very thing I craved: God's comfort.

Grief is not a weakness to be compensated for but rather an avenue of God's presence and transformation in our lives. Honesty about our discomfort allows us to receive God's comfort.

AS THE SUN LAUNCHED HIGHER off the horizon, drying the salty tear streaks on my face, I headed back down the beach.

Leaving my shame and performance behind, I slowly gave honesty a try. I began to tell God the things that had previously made me feel like a failure to say—things that, of course, He already knew but that I needed to take to Him nonetheless. I was hesitant at first. *What if my ugly feelings cause me to lose favor with God? What if He is disappointed that I am saying them out loud?* But this time my desire for connection with God became stronger than my desire to protect myself.

"Why? . . . I'm confused. . . . I don't think I can do this again. . . . Did I do something wrong? . . . Why didn't You intervene? . . . This doesn't make any sense and it feels unfair. . . . Is it because You don't think I will be a good mom? . . . Is there wisdom to take from this? If so, what is it? . . . I want to have a family so badly—how long will I have to wait?"

As I named my fears, my questions, and my desires out loud, I no longer saw God above me but beside me. I felt immediately comforted by the confidence that I am known by my God. He knows us, and He knows each of these fears, questions, and desires, spoken or not. But speaking them reminds us of this truth.

This is not a distant kind of knowing—knowledge that comes merely from being told. This is a knowing that He feels.

Christ identified and absorbed my suffering on the cross. He *knows* the brokenness I encounter and the emotional pain I carry.

As I neared our friends' beach home, I was still stricken with grief. But being honest about that allowed me to be comforted by His grace. And that made all the difference.

THE LADIES WHO LUNCH

THE FAILURE OF PRIDE

> *I think there's just one kind of folks. Folks.*
> —SCOUT IN HARPER LEE'S *TO KILL A MOCKINGBIRD*

I pulled into a narrow parking spot farther from the country club entrance than I would have preferred, given the pelting rain. The parking lot was packed. Apparently, when it came to luncheons, it was important to be fashionable but not fashionably late. I studied the grassy hill that stood between me and the dining room where the luncheon was being held, strategizing the quickest and least precarious route in the downpour. The situation was not helped by the fact that I had no umbrella and was not excited about looking like a drowned rat, especially at this event.

I breathed deeply, trying to still the kaleidoscope of butter-flies flapping about in my stomach, while chiding myself for being so nervous. Luncheons feel like middle school for grown-ups. I tried to encourage myself by remembering that I was an adult who was capable of conversation. I told myself that everyone was probably feeling the same discomfort I felt and that insecu-rity has many faces. I reminded myself that the best approach is always to focus on making others feel welcome and communicate that they matter by asking them questions about themselves. But not even this self-coaching could shake the deep sense of inferi-ority I had brought with me.

Luncheons were new territory for me. I ate lunch on a regular basis, but I didn't "lunch." These social engagements seemed to occur mostly in the springtime and to carry a flare of elegance, no matter what the cause or occasion. Some were invitation-only and exclusive. Some were held in country clubs or hotel ball-rooms. Most were fund-raisers. My nerves weren't helped by the fact that this particular event was known for being especially extravagant. Some people viewed their invitation as a confirma-tion of social standing, akin to the status some might feel having a particular degree or a leadership position in a club or social society. Despite my invitation, I felt terribly out of place, but I decided that I had no choice but to go inside.

I entered the building, and suddenly the scuffs on my flats seemed more noticeable than I had remembered. My fears about being underdressed were quickly confirmed. Again, I silently reminded myself of what mattered and made my way toward the registration table, grateful for a direction in the sea of unfamiliar faces. Every conversation I passed along the way seemed to focus on what people were wearing. Or worse, *who* they were wearing.

As I scanned the rows of nametags, I tried to think about how I could make Marshalls sound like a fancy designer.

I found my nametag quickly. When your last name starts with the letter *Z*, this is not usually a difficult task. After signing in and collecting my table number, I stood awkwardly in the corner of the large foyer and desperately looked for someone I knew. Hundreds of women stood in small, tight circles. I didn't see one group that I could break into comfortably. I once again tried to remind myself of my belonging even as I stood on the outside of the circles. But my self-talk soon gave way to pride. *Who do these women think they are?*

Before I could answer my own questions, I spotted someone I recognized in the far corner. I didn't know this woman well but was more connected to her than anyone else in this crowd. She was known and admired by many, a vision of beauty and smarts. As I made my way toward her, her eyes met mine. I smiled at her excitedly, waving and mouthing the word *Hi!* as I pushed through the crowd toward her. Coming closer, I could see that the look on her face didn't match mine. Her eyes had left my face and were now scanning the rest of me. Her expression fell to disapproval. She looked me up and down before offering a tight-lipped smile, her long eyelashes coming together with each slow blink. She turned in toward the circle, closing the gaps beside her.

My whole body felt hot, chilled, and sweaty at the same time. I was humiliated. My worst fears of rejection and a lack of belonging were confirmed. I tried to silence the lies—that I wasn't good enough for the circles and that I couldn't measure up to the standards of the place I was supposed to call home. But I was struggling to answer this pain with truth. With no one to talk to after retreating back to my corner, I had a conversation with myself.

What is wrong with these people?!

How is it acceptable to treat someone like that?!

They just don't understand what really matters.

Who would want to be like these women anyway? I'm so glad I'm not.

Because of the inferiority I felt, I had resorted to pride. Considering myself better than the people in the circles was my means of surviving the pain of being left on the outside of them. The only way this event would be acceptable to me was if they accepted me.

It was time to find our seats, and I was thankful for the structure the program provided. The small talk continued to erupt around me before the parade of speakers took their turn on stage. I'm not proud to confess the monologue that took place inside my head as each woman presented. *How can these women talk about God when their actions reflect nothing but superiority and exclusivity? They need to practice what they preach! Faith is just one more accessory they wear to look good. Their brand-name handbags might be real, but at least my faith isn't a knockoff!* I heard nothing but the prideful voice inside my head for the rest of the event.

A few days later, on Sunday morning, I found myself back in our usual seats in the front left section of the church, comforted by the familiar smiles and the rhythms and routine of the service. These were my people.

I had stuffed that luncheon in a box in my mind and tossed it in a pile of things I never wanted to do again. I dismissed it as one of those Fairfield County events that was the definition of everything that is wrong with this world. The pain of being snubbed by the woman I had previously called a friend went into the box too. *How could she?* If I wasn't good enough for the circles, they weren't going to be good enough for me either.

THERE'S A STORY IN ACTS 16 of Paul and Silas in prison, praying and singing praises to God (vv. 25–34).[1] It was nighttime, and an earthquake had broken the prisoners' chains. Assuming all of them had taken this opportunity to escape, the jailer drew his sword to take his own life. But Paul and Silas had not escaped. Instead, Paul spoke to the jailer, encouraging him not to harm himself.

What must it have been like for Paul to stand free of chains before the jailer—the man who was responsible for his captivity and had undoubtedly been quite cruel? The jailer, weak and vulnerable in the presence of his prisoners, prepared to kill himself, preferring this choice to the likely sentence of death that accompanied allowing prisoners to escape. It would have been easy for Paul to passively allow the jailer to follow through on this conclusion, guaranteeing his physical freedom. But Paul stopped the jailer from harming himself.

How do we apply Paul's response to the jailer to our reactions to people who oppose us? As a therapist, my ideas about forgiveness are based on theologian Paul Tillich's idea that forgiveness with integrity must hold a balance of love, justice, and power.[2] The pain of feeling insignificant often leads us to pursue power in isolation—even if only in our minds. We often cope with our own deep sense of inferiority by finding a sense of superiority through pride and judgment. How would we have reacted if we were in that jail cell instead of Paul?

THE TIME CAME FOR COMMUNION—a ritual we participate in every Sunday as a church body. I was scheduled to serve, which meant standing at the front of the church and handing each congregant who came forward a piece of bread torn from the loaf in my hands as I said, "This is the body of Christ, broken for you."

Rows of people lined up in the aisles as the worship band softly played "O Come to the Altar," reminding us that because of Jesus, freedom is our reality.

I looked up at the people standing in line to come forward, grateful to be reminded of this truth and thankful for the gift of *this* community. And then I saw her—the friend who snubbed me at the luncheon was standing in the center of my line, making her way toward me. She did not regularly attend my church, so her presence was unexpected. I panicked. One would think that a few days' time would have healed the wound her actions had left me with, but my feelings had remained raw.

I continued my duties as a Communion server while I pleaded with God.

Lord, help me. I do not want to serve this woman Communion. You know what she did to me! Please don't make me do this . . .

But now she stood before me, her eyes locked on mine and her hands open to receive. And as I watched the bread tear in my fingers, tears suddenly stung my eyes. My focus shifted from what she did to what Christ has done for both of us.

My eyes met hers once again.

"The body of Christ, broken for you."

And for me.

In my pride and judgment, I had sought refuge in keeping company with people who are like me, which allowed me to adopt an us-versus-them mentality. But there in the midst of the ritual that symbolized Christ's sacrifice, I had to remember that if Christ is for us, He must also be for *them*. If Christ is for me, He must also be for *her*. Communion is the most tangible reminder we have that there are no circles at the foot of the cross.

The piano slowed, and I took my seat once again. I now understood why Paul stayed and rescued his captor. The grace Paul had personally experienced through Jesus Christ in his own life shaped the way he saw the man most people would have considered an enemy. The miracle of the broken chains in prison was a mere reflection of the miracle of Christ's death and resurrection. Paul and Silas carried that miracle in their hearts—even in prison. To merely enjoy their outward freedom would have been selling themselves and the jailer short of the inner freedom we can only experience through Jesus Christ. Through Jesus, Paul could see the jailer not as a ticket to freedom but as a man in chains in need of freedom himself.

JESUS EXTENDED HIS HAND across the boundary lines we tend to draw between ourselves and the people we've decided are the enemy in our own minds and hearts: Democrats and Republicans, *that* church versus *our* church, one racial group versus another, the disruptive woman at the Bible study, the neighbor who does everything wrong. In doing so, Jesus challenges us to see people we have difficulty loving as He sees them.

Was God asking me to view this woman differently? How was the failure of pride allowing me to see this woman more accurately? On the surface, this woman was the picture of freedom. She had financial security, a manicured image, and opportunities to pursue at her leisure. I couldn't detect the pain in her life, but I also knew that unkind behavior doesn't happen in a vacuum; it is always rooted in pain. She displayed the image of freedom, but I wondered if her heart was held captive.

I, too, am a person in need of rescue, and that reality leads me to confront my own destructive tendencies. Someone else's pain might come in different packaging. But I know what it's like to do harmful things when I hurt. If we're honest, we all do. This understanding doesn't excuse the harmful behavior, but it does help me have compassion on the heart behind it—a heart I recognize looks a lot like mine.

When you decide that there is no "us" and there is no "them," you'll start to see that to be human is to be in need of Christ's finished work on the cross. And you will see that our personal need is equal to that of anyone standing around us. Pride provides an illusion of uneven ground—a picture that tells us that some of us need more grace than others. But the cross levels that ground and erases the lines we love to draw to make ourselves feel just a little bit better and less needy than the people we struggle to stand next to. Maybe the woman who left me outside the circle was not my enemy or the obstacle to my freedom but rather my sister standing on level ground at the foot of the cross.

THE FINAL SONG OF THE SERVICE played, and the congregation rose to their feet to scatter into the rest of their Sunday. I spotted the woman standing at the back of the room.

The band played on, singing the words of a reprise of "O Come to the Altar" with conviction and reminding me that all of us are in need of the forgiveness purchased with the blood of Christ.

The body of Christ broken for *both of us*. The blood of Christ shed for *both of us*.

Like control, perfectionism, and performance, pride is a habitual shield against my deepest pain. Your wounds and shields might have different names, but they, too, have well-worn paths in your mind and heart. They are as familiar to you as the patterns on the palms of your hands. But after a while, we realize that we were not made for what feels most familiar. We were made to be free.

BREAKING DOWN
DISCUSSION QUESTIONS

1. When you feel emotional pain, what do you find yourself doing to protect yourself?
2. How did you learn these protective behaviors?
3. How do people typically respond to you when you engage in these behaviors?
4. How do these methods of protection ultimately keep you from experiencing peace and joy?
5. What are some limitations you experience? How might these ultimately serve as a vehicle of freedom?
6. How have you seen God's story through others' willingness to share their own stories?
7. When have you experienced connection through vulnerability?
8. When has honesty about your discomfort allowed you to receive comfort from God or others?
9. What person or group of people do you struggle not to see as your enemy? How is God inviting you to see them as a person or people in need of rescue instead?

PART 3

BREATHING IN

FINDING A LASTING PEACE

CHAPTER 10

HOME

FINDING REFUGE

*The real settling will be to settle more and more
deeply into the heart of Jesus.*

—HENRI NOUWEN

W ell, I guess these belong to you." Our Realtor flashed
a cheesy grin as he dropped a set of house keys into the
palm of Jimmy's hand. We both laughed nervously, aware of the
responsibility that came with this tiny set of keys. It was May 5,
Cinco de Mayo, and we were closing on our first home. The
only thing we knew about home ownership was how much we
did not know.

It was difficult to absorb the fact that the house was actually ours. We had been searching earnestly for quite some time and didn't anticipate that this dream would happen for us for several years. Real estate agents who were tasked with selling homes in our price range seemed to either advertise the home's potential or cater to developers who would be interested in simply knocking the structure down and starting over, which seemed to be the most logical solution in some cases we had seen. Most of the houses we were shown smelled of animals that had long since passed and featured carpet that could tell stories about the Kennedy administration. Other real estate agents found elements of these homes to highlight for the buyer. My favorite to date was the home that boasted "territorial views," which meant that one could see the mailbox from the front window.

In an act of defiance against our budget, I toured our little gray Cape Cod–style home during an open house one Sunday in January when Jimmy was out of town on business. Wandering from room to room, I wrote this home's next chapter to include us. Upon leaving, I promptly sent Jimmy a text that I found our house. He laughed when I told him the price, but I was undeterred. I convinced him to put in an offer, which we did with a hope and a prayer. On the morning we planned to submit our offer, the sellers dropped their price significantly, taking our offer from offensive to aggressive.

After a tumultuous negotiation process and a comedy of errors on the part of the seller's agent, the house was ours. Circumstances had made it very clear that this house was a pure gift from God.

I loved our little house on the corner. I could see my life dance in its rooms. I could see our newly formed small group standing around the kitchen island, sharing the made-from-scratch baked goods they'd brought and laughing together over gorgeous sour-dough or sea-salted fudge. I would likely be joking about how I slaved all day on something I scratched the price tag off of five minutes before everyone arrived. As inspiring as this sweet white kitchen was, I couldn't help but feel like it was being wasted on the wrong person. I am not much of a cook, but it was a nice room to look at.

In the living room, all I could focus on was the fact that the room had a fireplace—the answer to our Connecticut winter woes. I could see the corner where I would write and sip coffee, and the coffee table where our future kids could drive their toy cars back and forth across the surface.

Wandering upstairs, I recognized the square room in the corner as the nursery for the baby we had just found out was on the way. After the miscarriage a few months prior, the nursery was a fun and tangible way to look to the future with hope. We didn't know yet whether the room should be decorated in pink or blue, but perhaps I would just make it blue. I was never really a person who cared for the color pink.

I could hear the songs that would be sung in this room—songs from the archives of my own childhood that my parents sang to me as a little girl. I didn't even know the names of the songs, but the lyrics and the truth inside them were the building blocks of my childhood. I could see the books—*The Little House, Goodnight Moon, Blueberries for Sal*—scattered across the wood floors and blanket forts in the corners. This was our house.

Climbing back into the car, Jimmy interrupted my thoughts by suggesting a celebration dinner at Chipotle. I laughed, catching his hint that, having just left our savings account on the third floor, we would be going with the budget option for our Cinco de Mayo dinner this year. After picking up two burrito bowls to go, we stopped by our rental cottage to grab a bottle of champagne we had been saving for a special occasion. Of course, Jimmy was the only one who could drink it, but I didn't care. It felt festive and fitting for the celebration.

We unlocked the front door, grinning at each other in disbelief. Hungry and wasting no time, we sat down on the dining room floor and toasted with Jimmy's champagne and my S.Pellegrino in clear plastic cups, feeling nothing but gratitude for this space we now called home.

I insisted on sleeping in the house on the first night. As I lay awake in my sleeping bag like the Girl Scout I never was, I felt the full weight of our decision to purchase a home. Putting down roots in Connecticut was in direct conflict with the daydreams I had indulged since moving here two years prior. I spent most of my time imagining our life elsewhere. My mind was a constant flight risk, making it difficult to properly invest in relationships and the possibility of a future here. I gazed at the ceiling and wondered what light fixture we could find to replace the one I was staring at.

For most of my time as a resident of the Northeast, I realized I had been using the environment around me. I was more interested in what I could take from our time here rather than asking myself how I could give of myself to this place. I had been more focused on what I had lost and left behind in California than on seeing the joys that were waiting to be found here in Connecticut. This house would change all that, serving as a tangible reminder that we had a future worth investing in *here*.

SOMETIMES WE READ JEREMIAH 29:11 and, because of its familiarity, assume it has nothing for us. But the prophet's words are deep and rich with meaning: "'I know the plans I have for you,' declares the LORD, 'plans to prosper you . . . plans to give you hope and a future'" (NIV).

Previously I have understood this verse to be an encouragement that even when our reality looks different from our dreams in the moment, our prosperous plans are promised for the future. And though we may have to wait, God does understand the life we long for and has plans for us that match the dreams we carry.

But the verses surrounding Jeremiah 29:11 tell a different story. When God spoke these words, the Israelites were in exile, calling a land they did not love "home." In this particular passage we find them spending their time waiting for better days to come. They camped, but they did not live. They engaged only with themselves, hiding out among like-minded people. They did nothing to bless their neighbors or influence the culture around them. This approach was reinforced by false prophets who had told them that the days they dreamed of were just around the corner, which only served as further encouragement to put the business of living and blessing their neighbors on hold.

We can easily find ourselves camping instead of living. I recognized myself as someone who was at risk of wasting the opportunity to find the gifts of the present in Connecticut as I waited for better days in the life I could so easily envision elsewhere.

The prophet Jeremiah confronted the Israelites' lack of engagement by telling them to plant fruit trees—an investment that might not yield fruit for years. He told them to build houses and settle down. His instructions were an invitation to stop waiting for better days and to live in *these* days in *this* place. Jeremiah also called them to "seek the welfare of the city" (29:7 ESV). He challenged them to not hide among themselves but to engage with their neighbors and influence the culture around them.

These seemed like odd instructions leading up to verse 11, which had always brought so much comfort. How could God's promise of prosperity and a hopeful future be found in a life they did not choose?

Many times in Scripture, God Himself claims to be our home—our shelter. The Israelites may not have chosen their reality, but God was their connection between reality and a kind of prosperity that surpasses what we can dream of. Seasons of exile, seasons we would not choose for ourselves and that do not match our dreams, are the seasons when we remember our home is in Him—a Person who cannot be taken away from us. Perhaps the prosperity that Jeremiah was referring to was the transformation that can only come through finding our secure home in Christ. And maybe it is only when we are changed that we can change the world around us.

THERE'S A HOME VIDEO OF one of my first Easter egg hunts, when I was two years old. I was obsessed with the color purple at the time, and it is clear from watching the video that I was most intent on finding the purple plastic eggs. Toddling across the uneven lawn in my shiny Mary Janes, I would pass dozens of other colored eggs, full of treats and treasures, as I pursued the one prize I had in mind. Perhaps my instincts have not changed. I didn't want to miss finding the gifts that God is freely offering just because they look different from what I had imagined. Yet again, was I at risk of missing the miracle of the manna?

As much as I loved this house, the decision to plant roots in Connecticut was not the picture of the hopeful future I had been carrying in my mind these past couple of years. But this is what I've learned the hard way: we find exactly what we look for. Often, it's the places outside of our comfort zone that make us hungry for a Home that does not change. And time and time again, I have found that it's the people and cultures that are different from ourselves that have something important to teach us, leaving us changed for the better.

The gifts aren't difficult to find once you decide to look. In the last couple of years, I found precious friends I never would have met if we had not made the decision to move. I saw new growth in myself that came from the pruning of old behaviors that were not serving me and were never meant to work. I discovered more about the character of Christ and a new trust in Him. These are treasures I have found not in spite of Connecticut but because of Connecticut—because of *these* days and *this* place.

There are gifts waiting to be found in your life too. To find them, though, you have to decide that your life is happening now, not someday. You might feel as though you can enjoy your life only when you achieve a particular goal, when you hone a certain skill, when you can buy the thing you've been saving for for years, or when your family is complete. But like me, you'll run the risk of missing the joy of living here and now. You'll miss the opportunity to invest in the lives of your neighbors—to be a blessing rather than a person biding her time. But when you see that these unwanted disappointments or seasons of waiting are opportunities to seek refuge in God, you'll find a peace you can take with you into every new place and season—a Home you never have to leave.

I turned over, weary from the internal wrestling and determined to find rest on the wooden floor. The nasal breathing and occasional soft grunts beside me were signs that Jimmy was sound asleep. Jimmy is a person who always rests well wherever he is. He seems to have eyes to see the joy regardless of his circumstances. I was happy to have a more permanent home. But I hoped that, as we continued to settle and make this house our own, I would never mistake the gift of this house for the comfort and contentment that only the person of Jesus Christ can give. As excited as I was about the fulfillment of this dream to own a home, I never wanted to trade God's plans for my cheap dreams. I hoped my soul would never cease to long for the place that I belong. In settling, I didn't want to lose my newfound sense of being sent.

CHAPTER 11

CALMED STORMS

FINDING PEACE

You find peace not by rearranging the circumstances of your life, but by realizing who you are at the deepest level.

—ECKERT TOLLE

The waiting room in the doctor's office looked like a DMV with carpet. Nothing had changed. The same receptionist sat behind the desk, hiding behind a glass panel and making calls as she smacked her bubble gum. The same maternity and newborn photos littered the office walls, advertising local photographers' work. And the same tattered parenting magazines were sprawled across the worn coffee table, boasting headlines like "How to

Stay Fit and Sexy While Pregnant." Personally, I would have been happy to be the size of a Sprinter van if it meant carrying a baby to term, but whatever.

Maybe this pregnancy will be different.

My legs crossed, top foot flopping up and down in nervous rhythm, I leaned back, squinting out the window and scanning the driveway, hoping to see Jimmy's car pulling in through the pelting rain. Having just landed at JFK Airport hours before, he wasn't sure if he would make the appointment. However, I wasn't sure if I could make it through the appointment without him.

I tried to calm myself by remembering that we had already heard a heartbeat—an improvement from the first time I was pregnant. And while the measurements looked to be a few days off, the doctor had assured us that this was common and gave us no reason to panic yet.

Yet . . .

"Nicole?"

The door to the waiting room flung open, and the ultra-sound technician ushered me into the room. I explained that my husband was on his way, and she kindly agreed to wait. I knew from experience that she had the warmth of a concrete floor, so I was grateful for the pleasant interaction. While I waited, I dressed in the flimsy robe and placed the paper sheet awkwardly over my lap as she occupied the uncomfortable silence by reviewing my ultrasound images from days before.

The small talk continued as my own heartbeat played double time. I had started to feel nauseous and shaky by the time Jimmy walked through the door, soaked from dashing through the rain and looking just as relieved to be there as I was to see him.

Seconds later, we were looking at the picture of the life I prayed was growing inside of me. And once again, I saw everything I needed to know on the technician's face. I knew right away she was searching for something that simply was not there. It was clear she really wanted to give me different news from what her face had already spoken.

"I'm so sorry . . . the baby's heartbeat has stopped."

With heaving sobs, I pressed my face into Jimmy's scratchy cheek, simultaneously comforted by the closeness and worried that a child may never know the comfort of this man's face. It was difficult to discern which tears belonged to Jimmy and which tears belonged to me. Time loses all weight in moments like this, and it felt like we stayed in that room longer than we should have. Finally, with heavy limbs, I managed to get dressed and somehow walked out of the office.

Having to leave and walk through a lobby of staring pregnant women is a special brand of torture. Some of the women glanced at me with knowing looks—as though they had been there before and were familiar with this specific sort of pain. Others squirmed and averted their eyes, as if I were contagious and my situation might infect theirs.

Jimmy and I have since learned that most other fertility and OB-GYN offices have a different exit for these kinds of situations—a special door for sad people like us. But no matter what door you walk through, you're still leaving feeling as if a necessary part of you is left behind, trapped on the inside. Inaccessible. The hope and excitement you should be carrying with you is replaced by a dream that has gone cold. Future dates that were supposed to have significance no longer do. Conversations with friends and family that you imagined having no longer make sense. Suddenly, you're free to go on that vacation or say yes to that speaking engagement, but you wish you weren't.

You have to carry this cold, lifeless dream; it feels both painful to let go of and painful to hold. As in all grief, walking through the recovery from a miscarriage is excruciating, cathartic, and necessary for healing all at the same time. In moments like these, it feels like an *out* is what you crave most. But the only sure route to the other side is through the grief. And there is no map for *through*.

As we walked toward our cars, I noticed people hustling around town as though today were normal. One woman had just loaded her farmer's market finds into her car. Another man collected his cash from an ATM. For some people, today was going exactly as planned, and everything they put effort and energy toward happened the way they wanted it to. But just as when you're sick and you can't imagine how anyone feels normal, I couldn't picture what it would feel like to do things like run errands and talk on the phone.

We decided to leave Jimmy's car in the lot. I was nervous about my ability to focus on the road, and I didn't want to be alone. Neither of us said much on the way home. *Whys* were wondered and *now whats* were asked, but no answers were offered. Still very much craving a way out, I typed *Seattle* into our GPS. If we just kept driving, exactly how long would it take to get back to a place that was familiar and comfortable and yet so "other" from where we were? It turns out that the familiar feeling I longed for was at least two days and seven hours away.

It was only ten o'clock in the morning when we arrived home, but I looked and felt like I do at the end of a long day. I put my pajamas on and robotically crawled back into bed. My eyes landed on the sonogram picture—the flimsy, blurry black-and-white photograph I had positioned carefully on my nightstand, poised to be prayed for. That picture had seemed so sure, representing the beginning of a story that would never be finished in this lifetime. I closed my eyes, hoping in vain to wake up to a different kind of day.

As it turns out, my miscarriages were not coincidental. A battery of fertility tests revealed we have a rare genetic abnormality for which there is no cure. This particular condition significantly reduces our chances of carrying a baby to term. Suddenly, statistics became our best subject. Questions like *What are the odds of getting pregnant?* and *How many times do we need to get pregnant to have the number of kids that we want?* were the main topics of conversation in our house.

Though this diagnosis was not news I would have chosen for us, having a known cause for this pain gave me a strange feeling of comfort and a false sense of control. When you have relied your entire life on grit and hard work to turn dreams into realities, you operate around the lie that you can do everything in order to feel as though you and your dreams are safe. In this case, safety looked like having the family I had always envisioned. I used the information we gathered at appointments to analyze our odds of carrying a baby to term, forcing my will back into our future. The waters may have been rougher than we had foreseen, but I could still steer this ship.

On a gray Sunday in December, I was unloading the dishwasher while my aimless mind settled on a conversation I had with a friend earlier that week. I had explained the information we had recently learned about our diagnosis in unnecessary detail and reported my predictions for what this would mean for us in the future. She listened and encouraged me, and just before we said goodbye, she said, "Well, Nicole, this sounds hopeful . . . especially when we know our hope is in God and not the odds."

The statement was meant to offer nothing but comfort, but I felt convicted by this truth I had forgotten. This simple encouragement exposed the fact that God had become a mere accessory to the strategy I had constructed in order to feel that my desires were safe in the hands of the future. God was never excluded from my longings or vision for my life, but the sobering reality was that I was more comforted by the supporting evidence than I was by Him.

I had misplaced God. I found myself repeating the prayer "My hope is in You . . . My hope is in You . . ." as both an acknowledgement of God's power and as a reminder to myself about where He belonged in the context of my dreams. While I was still doing calculations in an attempt to identify the various possibilities for having the family we had envisioned, my grip on my sense of control had slipped. What I had always known, but was just now seeing clearly, was that if we were going to have a family, God was going to be the one to give it to us—in His way and in His time.

Staring out my kitchen window, I watched the last leaves of fall cling in vain to the naked, spiny branches of winter. The trees were lit by the glow of white lights, celebrating the holiday season—a season that only intensified my longing for what could be and my pain about what was not.

I was halfway through placing our mugs back into the

cabinets when I paused and suddenly wondered how I would finish that sentence. *My hope is in God . . .* for what?

The answer was easy: a baby.

Though this was indeed true, I found it to be unsatisfactory. The answer to my pain was still the gift itself and not the Giver. Essentially, my prayer was, "My hope is in Jesus to give me the things that I want, which will bring me peace." I interacted with God as if He were merely the facilitator of my agenda or the power source for my plans. I was focused on what God could do for my story instead of asking Him to move through my story.

THE BOOK OF MARK TELLS THE STORY of Jesus and His disciples in a fishing boat during a terrible storm. The disciples were quite anxious, and when Jesus finally awoke, He seemed a little perturbed, or at the very least confused, by their anxiety and lack of faith (4:35–41).

When I read this story, I always feel a little defensive of the disciples. A life-threatening storm with a sleeping Savior in a tiny boat seems like a valid cause for worry to me—until I realize that like me, they just wanted to know that everything was going to turn out all right. Like me, they put their hope in the calmed storm instead of in the One who calms them. They were desperate for an *out*, missing the fact that Jesus was showing them a way *through*—a way through to peace outside of circumstance. His posture in the boat was not one of complacency but of extreme confidence in God—a God who is capable of intervening in ways that don't make sense to our human understanding.

In the same way, if someone could have shown me where

the emergency exits were located in my problem, I would have taken full advantage. But the absence of an *out* helped me slowly recognize the gift of sitting in the boat with Jesus in the midst of the storm. More than an answer to my desire, He was the answer to a deeper longing.

Walking this life with Jesus does not eliminate pain. The sting of losing another baby was sharp. The ache of another year passing without a change was real. The longing to be surprised by joy and the pang of disappointment that inevitably followed was excruciating. No, Jesus' presence does not eliminate our pain, but it does change the pain. We can be in pain and at peace at the same time. As Christians we hold the gift of knowing the end of the story—knowing that it is going to be okay. Because of Jesus' death and resurrection, we know that what is dark today will not be dark forever. We can hold confidence that God will not waste any earthly outcome—even if it is not the one we were hoping for.

Our culture would lead us to believe that the peace and joy we desperately search for is the fruit of a problem solved, a change of venue, or a dream realized. But I found that my longing connected me to God in ways that few things do. We need Jesus all the time, but painful moments give us the unique gift of *seeing* just how much we need Him.

LOOKING BACK ON MY LIFE, I can now see that every obstacle and interruption I faced came with an invitation to let Christ be my peace outside of circumstance. What we desire most is ultimately meant to usher us into a deeper intimacy with Him. Here, we realize that in our longing, the real gift is when our circumstances shape us into the likeness of Christ. I never thought the gift would look like this. I assumed that joy would follow a change from the outside, but the true joy was the change that was happening inside of me.

Sometimes the storm is calmed, and sometimes it seems to rage on forever. I don't understand why some diseases are healed and some are not, why some relationships are reconciled and others are left frayed and undone, or why sometimes we get to receive the dream and other times we are left empty-handed.

I find this part of life to be particularly confusing and messy, and I do not understand it. Sometimes God doesn't save us *from* the pain, but He always saves us *in* the pain. Sometimes we get what we are hoping for, and sometimes we don't. And sometimes we get something we never knew to pray for: the peace that comes from a deeper intimacy with Christ.

I remembered a text my friend Lauren had sent me in the wake of our difficult news weeks before. Tucked into her comforting words was Psalm 119:50: "Your promise preserves my life" (NIV). In the context of the wrestling now, I saw that no matter what the outcome of my story might be, His promises—not my perfect plans—would be my peace.

I was led to pray one more time, recognizing that prayer puts my worry in the right hands and reminds me to choose faith over the formulas that give the illusion of peace they cannot deliver.

I repeated my prayer: "My hope and peace is in You . . . not in what You can do *for* me, but *in* me."

CHAPTER 12

A BIGGER STAGE

FINDING GOD'S GLORY

God is forming us into a new people.
And the place of that formation is in
the small moments of today.
—Tish Harrison Warren

Scribbling careful notes in the margin, I made final adjustments to my presentation, which was to take place the following day. Though I was comfortable with public speaking and did it often, I reviewed each point for the final time, hoping that going over the material just once more would appease my nerves.

The breakout session on vulnerability and leadership I was scheduled to lead was for a regional youth workers' conference, with hundreds of youth pastors and youth volunteers from churches and para-church ministries in the Northeast attending. The fact that I was passionate about this subject matter should have been enough to put me at ease. But there was something about this particular presentation that felt different—more official.

Perhaps it was the fact that the conference was taking place in a different state, requiring me to travel, even if the travel time was little more than a two-and-a-half-hour drive. Or maybe it was the fact that I was staying in a hotel room, although there wasn't much that was intimidating about a Comfort Inn with a view of the Mobil gas station on the corner. More likely, it was the fact that this was a regional conference and felt more official than the evening talks I often gave at churches in my local community, where I had become quite comfortable and familiar with the audience. Whatever the reason, I felt pressure to communicate something profound and to deliver it well.

The past couple of years in many ways had been defined by my efforts to build a successful private practice as a marriage and family therapist. This is difficult to do under any circumstances but particularly challenging when you are starting in a place where you have no personal network. Nonetheless, I had managed to do it. I attended every training and earned every certification I could to ensure I was offering the best service to my clients and to build my credibility. I never missed an opportunity to network, hoping to make a name for myself.

I knew that my practice would not be built with my grit but instead by God's grace. Yet I hesitated to test that and had spent the past few years giving those old habits just one more try. The discipline and strategy weren't problems in and of themselves.

As usual, much of my motivation was the desire to achieve and be an influential person. But despite any impure motives, I was seeing results that were more beautiful and profound than I could have dreamed of.

The miracles I watched on the little brown leather couch in my office should have assured me that God was working through me and moving in the lives of my clients. Though it was difficult to see the movement at times, many of the individuals, couples, and families I was blessed to work with should have been evidence that what I desired most—to be used by God—was already happening. But these sacred moments were all wrapped in small packages—moments tucked within the therapy hour that took place in my tiny office, unseen by anyone other than me and my clients. It was difficult for me to see the significance of work that went unseen by others.

I loved my work as a therapist, but I craved the assurance that I had influence beyond the walls of my office. Tomorrow's speaking opportunity felt like a bigger stage—a chance to prove to others and myself that the work I was doing mattered and that I was indeed leaving a unique mark on the world.

I carefully placed my notes back in my folder and laid out my clothes for the next day. I giggled out loud, remembering my husband telling me that he had a similar routine as a young boy. Each night he would "make a man" on the floor, arranging each article of clothing exactly as it would be worn the following day. I "made a woman" on the narrow space of carpet next to the bed and tried to push back all the questions I had for tomorrow's self. *What if I bomb this? What if no one comes?* The "woman" who now lay flat on the floor had no answer for me, and I went to sleep, uncertainty hanging in the air.

The next morning at 10:30 a.m., I found myself standing at the front of the small auditorium, staring at my notes but not really reading them as I watched the door, praying that more people would enter. One of the conference facilitators nodded at me from the back of the room, cuing me to begin. My heart sank. It was indeed time for the breakout session to start, and the seats were only about a quarter full. The door closed. All of the attendees could have shared one limousine. I tried to swallow my disappointment that the size of the audience wasn't what I had hoped for. I attempted to silence the voice of shame in my head questioning why I couldn't attract a large crowd. I said a prayer and plunged into the topic of vulnerability and leadership, discovering once again that relief usually comes when we find the courage to begin.

Approximately halfway through my presentation, I illustrated one of my points with a story that included my reaching out to hold a friend's hand at a time when words had escaped me. As I continued my session, an elderly woman sitting in the third row on the far right side of the room caught my eye. Tears were steadily streaming down her face. I moved on to talk about our worthiness as human beings and what it means to be loved in our vulnerability instead of our abilities, but my eyes kept wandering back to the woman in the third row. Her tears persisted throughout the rest of the session.

When the time drew to a close and most of the attendees had left, a small line formed for individual questions. I noticed that the woman from the third row was there, firmly holding her position at the end of the line, insisting everyone else take his or her turn first. She clearly wanted to speak with me alone.

When it came time for her turn, it was just the two of us in the room. Her eyes met mine for a brief moment before darting away. She struggled to begin, and I nodded, hoping to communicate encouragement but not pressure. When she did manage to find the words, she began to share her life story—one that could be mostly characterized by homelessness and abuse. She told me stories of when she experienced harsh judgment and rejection—my own heart breaking a little more with each tale she told. As she proceeded to share more about her recent past, I silently wondered about what I had said during my talk on vulnerability and leadership that caused the steady stream of tears.

And then she answered me: "You have no idea what you did for that woman when you held her hand," she said, fighting for the words through her emotion.

I paused, waiting for more explanation. Admittedly, I was a little surprised by her emotion around such a simple gesture.

And then she hit me with this: "No one has ever held my hand."

I don't have a category for what I felt in that moment. I had no idea what to say. All the words that came to mind felt insufficient. But I did know what to do. I reached out and grabbed both of her hands and held them in mine. Her scarred and weathered skin confirmed the story she had just shared.

My cheeks were now wet, my face mirroring hers. I looked into her eyes, staring down the lies she had believed for far too long. I knew I was not powerful enough to right these lies with my own words. But with my heart lodged somewhere between my collarbone and my mouth, I almost choked on my own words as I managed to say, "I am so sorry for your pain, and it's my honor to hold your hand." And like the kid she never got to be, she lunged into my arms for a hug.

I decided to try to race the forecasted snowstorm back home and left the conference early. But just twenty minutes down the highway, the first flakes began to spiral and dizzy my view. A novice driver in the snow, I surrendered to the slower pace of traffic. I was fighting what my colleague refers to as the adrenaline drain—the feeling that usually occurs a couple of hours after a big event where all the nerves, focus, and anticipation drain from your body and leave nothing but exhaustion behind.

I was coming home with something different from what I went for. I had hoped this conference was my opportunity to share my message on a bigger stage. I had looked forward to the rewards of credibility and notoriety that I expected would follow this event. But as I braved the Boston winter roads and December flakes swirled, dancing to the tune of howling wind, I thought about what I had been given instead.

My disappointment with the small crowd was interrupted by the moment I had shared with the woman from the third row. Though my hands gripped the cold, smooth leather of the steering wheel, I could still feel her weathered skin against my palms. The vision of her tear-stained face was still clear in my mind.

Traffic slowed to a crawl as the snow persistently fell. Cars began to spin into medians and guardrails, mostly at slow enough speeds that the damage was kept to a minimum. I didn't dare turn on the radio, not wanting to risk any kind of distraction; I let my own thoughts fill the vacant space.

It was difficult to reconcile my expectations before the event with what was most meaningful to me now. If I measured the day by numbers, disappointment was the only logical response and failure was the only reasonable conclusion. But the moment I had shared with the elderly woman was telling me a different story, revealing the narrow ideas I have about influence and where God's glory can be found. I knew little about her story, but in her loneliest moments I saw God's persistent presence. In the hopelessness, I saw God's relentless rescue of her—and of you and me.

GOD'S LIGHT—HIS GLORY—peeks out from broken places, turning the heartache and imperfections in our stories into a vessel of light. That's what the glory of God's redemptive work can do. If you're like me, you have a habit of looking for God's glory in one place. Often, we miss the pleasure of seeing His glory because we assume it only looks one way: big moments, big sales, big dollars . . . we try to limit God to the confines of our worldly economy. We naively assume that God's most powerful movements happen only in the moments that look dramatic and impressive to us. We live from the idea that the size of the audience is directly related to the magnitude of the impact. But hearing one woman's story and holding her hand showed me something different. I had found God's glory—not in the faces of many but in the story of just one.

God gives us poignant hints of His economy all throughout the Bible:

- The creation of man from dust (Genesis 2:7)
- Enemies conquered with a jawbone from a donkey (Judges 15:15)
- A small stone to slay a giant (1 Samuel 17:49)
- Victory with a small army (Judges 7)
- A crowd fed with five loaves and two fish (Matthew 14:19–21)

Each of these stories echoes the truth that God can move significantly in the small. In the space of a breath, in the mundane motion, in the ordinary that often goes unseen, God moves with great impact.

How can I assume that God's movement is limited to what I can see with my human eyes?

We can so easily project our limitations onto the God of the universe. We look at dust and assume that God can make nothing from it. We look at insurmountable obstacles and decide that it is too much to ask God to find a way. We see overwhelming need and get anxious, presupposing that God cannot provide. We look at our own lack of competency and forget that it is in our dependency that God does His finest work.

Who was I to dismiss the events of the day as insignificant? How could I assume that God moves only on big stages? How could I consider my conversation with this precious woman and decide that God was not at work in powerful ways? I had been committed to the idea that bigger influence yields more fruit. But in the rubble of the lost hopes and expectations of that day, I found God's glory in a moment I might have previously dismissed as unimportant. I gained a new confidence in God's active work in our lives.

I MADE IT HOME TO A QUIET HOUSE. As was my usual ritual, I immediately changed into my pajamas, unpacked my small travel bag, and reflected. I had carried with me to Boston such a deep desire to make a meaningful impact. But in thinking about the dust, the jawbone, small stones, a tiny army, and a meager offering of bread and fish, I wondered if impact doesn't happen through the pursuit of influence but through the pursuit of God. When influence is the object of our pursuit, it's easy to measure our success in terms of numbers. But when we shift our focus to pursue God, we recognize that our responsibility is to be obedient, and God produces fruit that we could never make on our own.

It occurred to me that the loss of my expectations for the day and my failure to attract a large crowd cleared the space I needed to be able to find God's glory in the ordinary.

It was just days before Christmas. The snow accompanied me home and was now falling steadily outside. The only thing I had energy to make was tea. Drinking tea and watching the season's first snowfall felt both festive and restful.

As I sipped and stared outside, I noticed a faint reflection of our wooden nativity scene atop our dining room cabinet in the window. A baby Jesus, barely larger than my thumbnail, rested in a miniature wooden manger. This is the gift of His glory: Christ stooping to our broken world and our beat-up and weary selves. Emmanuel—God with us. In the quiet of the night, in the unassuming backdrop of a barn, our Savior—the greatest gift—was born. We need not look further than the manger for assurance that the magnitude of the moment doesn't determine the measure of the miracle.

CHAPTER 13

ENOUGH

FINDING ABUNDANCE

> *An infinite God can give all of Himself to each of*
> *His children. He does not distribute Himself that*
> *each may have a part, but to each one He gives all*
> *of Himself as fully as if there were no others.*
> —A. W. TOZER

Gentle breezes blew back and forth like a friendly game of tennis. My dear friend Lindsay and I sat on her front porch steps, watching the day make an attempt at spring. I had met Lindsay at our church's women's retreat a few years prior. A mutual friend introduced us to each other on a hunch that we were kindred spirits and would be close friends. Our friend was right.

Lindsay made me feel at home. Just being in her presence made me remember what matters and forget what doesn't. She's one of those rare souls who not only has the gift of hospitality but *embodies* hospitality. She didn't live far from my office, and every time I had a break in my therapy schedule that was longer than an hour, I would drive past the horse farms of backcountry Greenwich just to connect with her for a couple of hours.

The people strolling by boasted their warm-weather threads, doing their part to coax the season out of hiding. Long Island Sound lay flat in the distance, diamonds dancing on the waves in the sunlight.

I bounced Lindsay's eight-month-old baby girl, Grace, kissing the fuzz on the top of her head and inhaling that sweet baby smell that no one can seem to figure out how to bottle. When Lindsay was six months pregnant with Grace, I decided that I was going to be her godmother and told Peter and Lindsay that I would like for this to be the case. I realize this is not how the godmother selection process usually works, but my audacity was the fruit of being deeply known and loved in this relationship. And in this particular friendship, it worked.

As I snuggled with Grace, Lindsay's equally delicious three-year-old son, Isaac, gave me a first-rate education on the difference between a bulldozer and an excavator. Between truck facts, Lindsay and I took in the beauty of the early April day, sneaking in adult conversation where we could.

But the cheerful day was tinged with an ugliness I harbored inside. I tried to fully engage, asking her about the kids and Peter's new job. But as someone who wears her heart on her sleeve and her feelings on her face, I gave myself away like a toddler playing hide-and-seek.

"Hey . . . what's going on?" Lindsay's hand reached out—an extension of the compassion in her voice.

Before there were words, tears pooled in the rims of my eyes. I buried my face in my hands and cried for a few minutes. I made a few attempts at an answer, but the words left my lips without a sound.

Finally, it came to me. "I'm feeling jealous."

I wasn't jealous of Lindsay. I was struggling with envy toward a friend back in California who seemed to be living the life I desperately wanted for myself. She was a life-sized display of the dreams I feared would never come true for me. She was an accomplished writer. Both she and her home looked like they belonged on the pages of a magazine. And, as someone who was not even sure she wanted kids . . . *Surprise!* With an explosion of pink confetti, she had announced to social media accounts everywhere the night before that she was due to give birth to a baby girl in May.

The words tasted every bit as bitter as they sounded. In general, I was comfortable with vulnerability, especially the kind that was self-deprecating in some way. I felt free to talk about the ways I felt unable to measure up and my fears about the future. But after two miscarriages and months of negative pregnancy tests, confessing my jealousy was another level. It feels more acceptable to talk about why I don't feel like I'm enough than it does to talk about how threatening it feels that a friend has the life I want. What felt ugly inside looked every bit as ugly to me upon confession.

There was a part of me that was happy for my friend and her pile of blessings, but most of me felt like every present that was added to her stack of gifts somehow subtracted from my own—as if God were Santa Claus and could distribute only the gifts inside his bag. I knew He had to have a lot of blessings to give, but when I consider God's blessings as finite, it doesn't matter how big the number is. The supply seems scarce. More for someone else always means less for me.

Though I desperately wanted to be genuinely happy for my friend, her joy felt like an assault on my pain. The beauty of my story felt dimmed by the bright light of her impressive life.

I had believed the lie of scarcity—the belief that there is a finite, and therefore a short, supply. Scarcity demands answers to questions like "Is there enough?" and, more specifically, "Will *I* have enough?" But with these questions I'm learning that whatever "it" is, it's never enough.

Scarcity hisses fear that goes beyond counting blessings. It convinces us that we must seize every opportunity as it comes for fear that there may not be another in the future. Saying yes to an opportunity becomes more about capturing the chance rather than embracing it with open hands. Scarcity is firm in its belief that someone else's success robs us of the chance to succeed. And scarcity always demands a winner and a loser.

A significant part of my grief poured out of me from this scarcity mentality. This mind-set is a battleground for comparison, where a competitive spirit grows. When others succeed, I have difficulty being genuinely happy for them. I tend to hoard ideas and resources out of worry that they will be taken from me. I can be possessive of what I perceive to be mine. I often say yes to opportunities regardless of whether they are right for this season, panicking at the thought that I may never have another chance. Missing out on my own dreams becomes my worst fear.

There are many reasons I love Lindsay and treasure her

presence in my life. One of these reasons is that she is never afraid to tell me the truth on topics ranging from the fact that I snore (just a little bit) to the fact that I have a tendency to give other people too much power over how I feel. Lindsay listened with understanding eyes, and when I had exhausted my words on the subject of my seemingly perfect friend back in California, Lindsay looked into the distance as if she were carefully studying my friend on the other side of the country.

"I see beauty there," she acknowledged. I silently wondered where she was going with this. She paused, looked me straight in the eyes with both compassion and conviction, and said, "And I see beauty here too. I don't know how God is going to grow your family or what He has planned for your career, but I am confident it will be beautiful, and I will celebrate with you in whatever the joy looks like."

Her words spoke to the heart of my struggle. I hadn't actually believed the truth that beauty can live in multiple places. But her wise heart and keen eyes could see that blessing in one place does not rob blessing from another.

Lindsay continued: "Do you remember what you told me when I was pregnant with Grace and was struggling to imagine what it would feel like to go from loving one child with my whole heart to two children with my whole heart?" she asked.

I nodded, remembering our conversation.

"You told me that like God's love, my love wouldn't get divided but multiplied. The same is true for you."

I knew Lindsay was right. God's provision for my friend didn't lessen what He had in store for me. There is no need to look over our shoulders in suspicion that a friend's success might rob us of our dreams or change the sovereign stories that

God has written into our lives. Cheering others on in their dreams and celebrating their successes will not take away from experiencing our own. There is abundance for us in encouraging others.

GOD CONFIRMS HIS ABUNDANT LOVE in the stories that reveal His character throughout the Bible. We find one of the most impactful examples in 1 Kings 17:7–16—the story of the prophet Elijah and the widow of Zarephath.

God told Elijah to get up and go to Zarephath, where He promised there would be a widow who would provide for Elijah. Sure enough, Elijah met this widow, and he asked her to fetch him some water, which she did willingly. The water wasn't a threat to her survival. But when Elijah asked her for bread, she confessed her poverty to the point of near starvation.

Just as I would have been, the widow became nervous; her generosity toward the prophet of the God of Israel would come at great expense to her and her son. This gift would endanger her family's security. But Elijah assured her that God had promised that her meager amounts of flour and oil would sustain both her and her son through the drought, even in the midst of her sacrificial gift.

Still, the widow had to rely on faith alone as she made a biscuit for Elijah with what were her last bits of oil and flour. She had to trust the provision before she could see it for herself. His promise came with the assurance that God would provide in the midst of her sacrifice. God's provision toward one does not come at the expense of the other. He has the ability to care for both.

Our feelings of scarcity are related to our understanding of abundance. When I think of abundance, I tend to think of seasons in my life when I get to celebrate a yes, when I am the one who has been picked, when my efforts end in a goal accomplished or a dream realized, and when I feel like I have what it takes. These are earthly joys I would choose, which are often disguised as the answer to the scarcity I feel—areas of my life where I crave *more*.

Your heart might crave more of something else: more money to pay the bills, more countries in the world explored, more degrees earned. But the kind of abundance Jesus desires for us is not *more* of the joy that we would add to our wish lists but a *different* joy entirely. Earthly joys are dependent on circumstance. But Jesus doesn't simply give us more of what we want; he gives us something different: Himself.

He said, "I have come that they may have life, and that they may have it more *abundantly*" (John 10:10 NKJV, emphasis added). The Greek word for abundance is *hyperballo*, which means a joy that is unmatched and unrivaled by any other earthly joy that we might choose. It's a lavish inheritance in Christ.

No longer is our hope in the earthly evidence. No longer is our joy confined by our circumstances. No longer are the possibilities limited to what we can see. We no longer have to hold back. We can dream big! We don't have to fight with blame and control, or hide with shame and a numbing escape. Regardless of our situation, we are both loved and secure.

Abundance is not limited to times of surplus. Abundance is trusting God to provide for our needs and surrendering our desires to His will. It's offering our gifts and resources back to God and watching with expectation to see how He will move. Abundance comes in believing that the kingdom of God is not somewhere, someday. He is here, now. And abundance that brings joy for one never comes at the expense of another.

Trading what we have known for what we need always takes courage. In my head, I know that abundance is the better version of what I hope for when I maintain a scarcity mind-set. But choosing abundance where I am—even if nothing were to change—feels scary. I worry I won't have enough or that I won't be motivated to fight for my fair share. I fear that my version of "more" and God's abundance will not match, and it is difficult to trust that what I need is better than what I want.

LINDSAY HUGGED ME FOR A LONG TIME. I rested my head on her shoulder, grateful for who she is and the friendship we share, and wondered if perhaps it's times of scarcity that allow us to see abundance most clearly.

CHAPTER 14

GROWING

FINDING GOD'S GOODNESS

Your past mistakes, your story, your heartache,
your circumstances, and the tension you feel right
now in your season—every bit of it is part of your
growing ground.

—LARA CASEY

Grabbing fistfuls of dirt, I bent low over my work, focusing on the spacing of each flower and vine as I planted our front porch flowerpots and window boxes for the spring season. My eyes feasted on the contrast of the bright spring-green potato vine against the regal purple verbena. We had just returned from the local nursery, where we had shopped alongside every other family in town. Apparently Mother's Day weekend is a popular time to plant in New England because frost is no longer a threat in mid-May. I also imagined that this day provided an excuse for moms everywhere to play the Mother's Day card and recruit extra help for their landscaping visions and endeavors.

I had been dreading this day all week. Our church has a beautiful tradition on Mother's Day in which every woman gets a rose whether they are a mother in their home or in their heart. For some, the bloom is the most real part of being a mother. But the thorn was the element of the rose that I identified with the most. It was difficult to see the beauty in this season of longing.

After finishing the first window box, I stood up to stretch my back and stared at my hands, noticing the dirt caked thick under my fingernails. A longtime seeker of colorful beauty, I reflected on the fact that it's easy to focus on the flowers and dismiss the dirt—the rich vessel of so much growth and splendor.

Moving on to the next window box, I remembered a conversation I'd had the previous year with my close friend Barb about her own garden. She had planted a large fruit and vege-table garden in the side yard of her house and recruited help from experts to teach her about the nuances of gardening and give her instructions for tending to each plant in various conditions throughout the season. She felt excited to grow vegetables, but the main objective was to grow one particular fruit, which was clear even in the garden's construction. All the other beds were carefully arranged around the large central bed that hosted the crowning jewel: the strawberries.

Barb did everything right throughout the season to ensure that the strawberries would flourish. She researched standard practices for various climate conditions. She consulted with master gardeners and followed their instructions to help the crop thrive. She learned that strawberry vines tend to wander and need to be placed back in the bed on a regular basis, which she did diligently. She shielded the crops from the harmful elements whenever she could. And she took all the necessary measures to protect the crop from critters.

Early in the season it appeared the crop was off to an auspicious start. On strawberry plants, flowers are an indication of fruit to come. Barb's vines were covered in tiny white flowers—a promising sign. Barb and her family were leaving for vacation for a week, and before she left she carefully placed netting over the strawberries to prevent bugs and animals from snacking on the crop.

It was an unusually rainy week in Connecticut—and Barb returned to a bumper crop of moldy strawberries.

I recalled Barb sharing with me how disappointed she was—frustrated that she had done everything right and that her efforts had failed to yield her the results she was hoping for.

But I can still see her face as she looked at me and said, "But I didn't lose the entire garden, just one fruit. Once I accepted the loss, I had eyes to see the beauty and was able to enjoy what was right in front of me the whole time."

I wondered if there was goodness in my own life that I was tempted to reject because it didn't match my expectations. I considered this past season—not the spring season, but the time that had passed since we moved from California. My faith had lost all its props. My manufactured securities were nowhere to be found. And when faced with pain, my old ways of protecting myself failed. But like Barb said about her garden, accepting the loss of things that were never meant to bring me peace and joy was allowing me to find the goodness of God that was right in front of me the whole time. And I almost rejected it. In fact, I regret to say there were many days when I tossed it aside as no good, failing in the face of challenge to recognize my new relationship with Christ for the gift that it was. This season looked very much like plain dirt, but God had been tending to the soil, allowing it to rest and preparing it for growth and blossom that was beyond what I could have hoped for. And I nearly missed it.

THE BOOK OF ECCLESIASTES holds the tension between the difficult reality of this life and the assurance of God's goodness. It challenges us to see the beauty in both the dirt and the bloom. The author Solomon prompted us to find goodness beyond what we can see. More specifically, in Ecclesiastes 3:1–9, Solomon discussed the mystery of seasons and presented this idea in the form of a ledger that could be interpreted as positive on one side and negative on the other.[1]

> There is an occasion for everything,
> and a time for every activity under heaven:
> a time to give birth and a time to die;
> a time to plant and a time to uproot;
> a time to kill and a time to heal;
> a time to tear down and a time to build;
> a time to weep and a time to laugh;
> a time to mourn and a time to dance;
> a time to throw stones and a time to gather stones;
> a time to embrace and a time to avoid embracing;
> a time to search and a time to count as lost;

a time to keep and a time to throw away;

a time to tear and a time to sew;

a time to be silent and a time to speak;

a time to love and a time to hate;

a time for war and a time for peace.

What does the worker gain from his struggles?

For most of us, it's easy to find goodness in the harvest—in the planting, in the birth of new life, and in the embrace. Personally, I find it too easy to stop there—to assume that anything good will be found on the bright side of the ledger and that the other side is to be survived and has nothing to offer me. I echo the question Solomon posed at the end of this passage: "What does the worker gain from his struggles?" Where is the goodness in another painful Mother's Day? What does one gain from the heartache of divorce? Where is the beauty in the loss of a loved one? These are just a few examples of the questions we can ask about the dark side of the ledger—the painful seasons in our lives.

I took another look at the dirt that almost covered my hands and forearms, dark and muddy. The dirt itself may not be beautiful, but it has purpose. It is a vehicle for both nourishment and growth. In my experience, God reaches us and nourishes us in different ways during seasons we are tempted to call "ugly." And the most beautiful growth often sprouts from those seasons we don't prefer.

I wonder if there is goodness to be found in any season that cultivates growth. I wonder if every season is a crucial part of what Lara Casey calls "your growing ground."[2] This does not mean that we won't walk through periods of time on the dark side of that ledger and stand confused. This truth doesn't guard the future with guarantees against pain or loss. Solomon himself said a few verses later that "no one can discover the work God has done from beginning to end" (v. 11). Yet we can find goodness on both sides of the ledger because every season is an opportunity to know God more fully. Therefore, every season carries an invitation to worship.

As I planted, something about touching and seeing and being a part of creation reminded me of what God intended for us: to be in relationship with Him and to grow into His likeness. Reflecting on the dark times and the times of celebration in my life, I could see where every season had drawn me into deeper relationship with my Creator. Embracing both sides of Solomon's ledger was allowing me to see that indeed both sides are vital—that the good life isn't a life without challenges but a life of growth and intimacy with Christ.

Sometimes our circumstances make us aware of what kind of season we are in. However, most often we let life happen without taking inventory of what kind of season we are experiencing. What name would you give the season you are in? Where would you place it on Solomon's ledger? Is this a season of birth and harvest? Or is this a season that looks like tearing down and searching?

I will not dismiss the pain that often comes with the tearing down, or the fear that can accompany the searching. But if there is goodness on both sides of the ledger, then there's an invitation for you in your season too. Could it be that the tearing down is making room for something new to be built in your life or even in your heart? Is it possible that, like me, you've been searching in the wrong places for the love and security your heart craves, and that this season has you searching for a Love that will finally sustain? Maybe this season that looks like plain dirt is fertile soil for new growth and beauty in your life.

Even the changing seasons can be unexpected and painful, shifting without our consent. But the changing seasons that lead us to a steadfast God change something in us. They grow us. And where there is growth there is goodness. Every season is a gift. We can try to build our lives, manufacturing our own goodness. But true goodness is found in surrender to God in any season, as He is the only one who can truly make anything grow.

We can be quick to rescue one another from the dark seasons. We explain them away with platitudes or try to construct comfort that keeps us numb to the transformation of a given season. We mean well, but I'm wondering if we are cheating each other from a season in which God has something profound for us. We don't need rescue from the pain as much as we need the growth that can come only from weathering the seasons that help us know more of God and grow in our relationship with Him.

I PLACED THE LAST VINE in its designated spot and admired the beauty spread before me. My tiny boxed garden was reminding me that there is a time to wait, a time to rest, a time to work, and a time to harvest and enjoy. Certainly I experience these seasons differently, but I now know that each season cultivates goodness, if we are willing to notice. This is my season to plant, and I'm making a place for seeds of hope, trusting that growth can occur in any kind of ground. And I am determined to watch the goodness grow.

BREATHING IN DISCUSSION QUESTIONS

1. Think about the painful messages you carry about your significance and security. What do you think God would say in response to those messages? What message of truth do you have for that hurting version of yourself?

2. What truth have you discovered about God in the midst of pain you would not choose?

3. Describe a season of exile or a moment of living outside your comfort zone in which God became your refuge in a new way.

4. When have you been tempted to place your hope in a solution rather than the Savior?

5. How have you seen God's glory in the ordinary in your life?

6. When have you been tempted to dismiss His glory because it came to you in a moment that felt small or insignificant?

7. Describe a time when it felt as though someone else's joy robbed you of yours. How have you experienced God's abundance in seasons of scarcity?

8. What is the goodness you have found in your own life on both sides of the ledger that Solomon described in Ecclesiastes 3:1–9 (see chapter 14)?

PART 4

LOOKING UP

CHOOSING JOY OUTSIDE OF CIRCUMSTANCE

CHAPTER 15

SATURDAY

CHOOSING HOPE

In the struggle lies the joy.
—MAYA ANGELOU

Our plans for the day had been canceled, as they always are when it snows in the Northeast. It was the day before Easter, and I sat in the room in the left corner of the second floor of our house and scribbled the mess inside myself onto a page, desperate for hope—and assurance of that hope—as I pleaded with God for a baby.

We had called that room "the nursery" since I strolled through the open house "just for fun" the previous January. After two miscarriages, I had moved my writing materials and a forty-three-dollar IKEA desk into the space to be used as a temporary office. But we still called the room "the nursery." Despite our grief and fear, I suppose this spoke to our real hope that someday things would be different.

Outside the nursery window the "storm of the century" raged on. The snowflakes flew sideways like a swarm of bees fleeing their disturbed hive. If you heard the news report on Channel 12, you might think the Empire State Building would be buried in snow by the end of Tuesday. It didn't appear to be quite the storm it was predicted to be, but I was thankful for the pause. New Yorkers and Fairfield County folk are not practiced in taking pauses.

Filling the blank space on my page, I sat hyperaware of any sign of new life growing inside me. I've learned that the problem with Google is that everything means something and nothing means anything when it comes to searching for signs that you are pregnant. But I sneaked searches anyway, looking for information that affirmed my hope. I found myself delighted by symptoms that were anything but pleasant. Just that morning I had caught myself giving the air a fist pump when I awoke feeling like I'd just returned from a month-long cruise.

I have found this to be true about hope: we look for assurance in the strangest of places. Searching for hope felt like hunting for a contact lens in the snow. I didn't know where to look inside myself to find it. I wasn't even sure if there was any hope left in me to be found. Quite frankly, I had no idea why I was interested in searching for it anyway. In some ways it felt fruitless, given that hope alone could not and would not change my situation. What was the purpose of looking for something that had no real value?

Maybe there was something about hope that felt fun—like even the slightest of possibilities provided something to look forward to. Though there may have been an element of excitement in hope, it mostly felt like a free fall into fear—a place of flailing uncertainty suspended between the grief of yesterday and the longing of tomorrow. It felt too vulnerable to ask for something without knowing if the answer would be yes or no.

IN THE FIRST CHAPTER OF LUKE, we read about the angel Gabriel visiting Zechariah and telling him that after years of his wife, Elizabeth, being unable to conceive, and in spite of their old age, they would have a son whom they would call John. Gabriel told Zechariah, "There will be joy and delight for you, and many will rejoice at his birth" (1:14).

I can only imagine that in the face of the facts and his personal experience, Zechariah felt this happy news was too good to be true. He heard the very promise he had always longed to hear, and yet he couldn't trust it. He replied, "How can I know this?" (v. 18). His focus on his own reality left him demanding assurance before he was willing to take a chance on hope.

Gabriel answered his plea by describing who he was and the God he served: "I am Gabriel, who stands in the presence of God" (v. 19). He answered Zechariah's doubt not with reason or argument but by telling Zechariah *who he was.*

This is my struggle too. Like Zechariah, I want to know how the story is going to turn out before I go through the vulnerability of believing. Faith felt more confident—safer somehow. But hope felt like a risk—always accompanied by the possibility of disappointment.

Uncertainty in our circumstances naturally leads us to want to let go of hope. Choosing to dwell in our current reality without expectation or hope for a change in our situation may feel like the best way to protect ourselves from pain. If we expect nothing, how can we be disappointed? If we prepare for the worst, maybe we will be ready if it happens. If I expect another month to end with me staring at a negative pregnancy test with one lonely, pink line or another pregnancy to result in miscarriage, maybe I can keep myself numb to life's disappointments. If one is trying to avoid a fall, it seems like the most prudent action to take is to stay low to the ground—to keep our hearts emptied of expectation.

As someone who has watched me try to protect myself from pain for years, my mom has named this personal strategy "practicing disappointment." This is different from *experiencing* disappointment. As human beings, none of us are immune to experiencing personal failure or disappointing outcomes. But for me, practicing disappointment is an attempt to control my circumstances and the resulting emotional pain by choosing it before it can choose me, similar to my habit of rejecting others before they can reject me. This strategy claims that if I wriggle myself into a position where I expect to be disappointed and do not allow myself to hope, I can only be surprised by joy.

Hope may leave us open to the possibility of experiencing disappointment, but choosing hopelessness as our default guarantees the very pain we are trying to avoid. Refusing to hope locks in the very darkness we fear. Denying hope that our circumstances will change prevents us from seeing any movement or joy at all. Choosing to believe we are beyond hope keeps us from pursuing any kind of growth.

This strategy does not come with a filter. If we attempt to

protect ourselves from pain, we protect ourselves from the joy too. We guard ourselves from the intimacy in relationship, blind to the opportunities to grow through what we must go through, and numb to the warmth of God's faithfulness even in the bleakest of seasons.

Despite my attempts to protect myself, I noticed my heart leaning toward hope for reasons I'm still not sure I understand. I could not quiet the longing within me—a search for a reason to hope that was beyond what I could see in the present moment. The search itself gave testimony to a belief that in the midst of my pain, there was something of value worth finding. The desperation in my heart spoke confidence that my current circumstances were not the end of the story. In the face of my situation, somehow, I was drawn toward the possibility of what God could do in my life.

Lamentations 3 makes the claim that there is not only a reason to hope but that hope is a good idea. The book begins with the raw and honest feelings that accompany grief and pain. But there is a turning point at Lamentations 3:21 when the author wrote, "Yet I call this to mind, and therefore I have *hope*" (emphasis added). The shift from despair to hope is not a result of miraculous intervention or a change in circumstance or venue. Hope comes as a result of a choice—a decision to trust the faithfulness of God beyond what can be found in our personal experiences.

The author of Lamentations was able to recall God's faithfulness throughout the generations that came before him and trust the God he knew beyond what he felt. This search for hope beyond what can be seen does not necessarily lead us to a different answer, but it does lead us to the steadfast character of God.

The veracity of His promises doesn't hinge on my circumstance, and it doesn't hinge on yours either, different as your situation may be from mine.

I never thought of hope as a choice. It felt like the fruit of a win or an answered prayer. Two Christmases ago, I stood at the dishwasher and acknowledged that my hope was in God. But I failed to fully recognize that it was already mine—if I was willing to choose it.

I had a conversation with a friend several years ago around this theme of hope. Life had left her feeling hopeless and worried about an uncertain future. Knowing her story, these feelings were understandable. I would have felt the same way. At the end of the conversation she said, "But what am I going to do? This is my life. This is my new normal." I didn't have the understanding back then to tell her what I would tell her now: Yes, your feelings are real. They might even overwhelm you and be difficult to speak into at times. But whether hopelessness becomes our new normal is up to us. We get to choose hope. Hope is available to everyone right now.

This idea may seem naive or grandiose. You might be thinking: *You have no idea what I've been through.* And you would be right. I don't. But I do know that our pain can't change His promises. I know that, because of Jesus, choosing hope is a brave decision that won't disappoint. And I can confidently say that hope is a choice available to you and me right now, regardless of what our circumstances might say, simply because of who God is.

I am comforted by a God whose character is immutably good. This fact alone makes choosing hope a good idea. But tears welled in my eyes as I sat in that empty nursery and tried to muster the courage to ask God for what I hoped for. I wasn't sure I could show up to ask God for my heart's desire one more time. Hope may be a good idea, but it felt safer to be quiet about it. And if my own life experience is all I chose to look at, it would probably be advisable to stop asking. After all, isn't that the definition of insanity—doing the same thing over and over again and hoping for a different result?

Asking God for what we hope for exposes us to the elements of disappointment and rejection. If you've only known relationships that hurt, it might feel scary to hope for a healthy one. If you've been rejected from more job opportunities than you can count, it may feel silly to ask God for the right position for you. Certainly God can and does move in our lives, and so many of us have stories of breakthrough—testimonies to His faithfulness. But we don't ask because it guarantees a change in our circumstances. We ask because it changes us. We hope not because of what we receive but because of Whom we receive regardless of the outcome.

Clinging to hope and making our requests known to God transforms us because we are making a statement about what we believe to be true about God. Simply asking the question claims the truth that the promises of God are real, regardless of the answer that we receive. In God's economy, a no is not a reason not to ask tomorrow. This is where I find the courage to ask one more time.

THE NEXT DAY, Jimmy and I would gather with friends and our church community to celebrate Easter—the day that changed everything and gave us a reason to hope. But as I sat in that quiet nursery on Easter Saturday, I wondered how the disciples must have felt the Saturday after Jesus' death, reeling from the grief of yesterday with no promise of tomorrow. Did they hope for a change? Was there a reason to hope?

It occurred to me that my Saturday—the space between the pain of yesterday and the promise of tomorrow—was an entirely different kind of Saturday than what the disciples experienced that day after Jesus' death, with nothing but grief and uncertainty as their companions. If my personal experience was all there was, hope would be a gamble at best. But it's not all I have. I know—we know—how the story ends. The entire Bible is testimony to God's steadfast love and faithfulness, and we sit in the privileged seat of knowing what happened on the third day—and what will happen on the last day. Jesus' death and resurrection gave us the gift of knowing that the darkness will lift. We can feel confident that what we can see is not all there is. The presence and person of Christ is the only safe investment for our hope.

Jesus' resurrection on that Sunday changed our Saturdays. When Christ conquered death, He made hope a good idea. It means that in the midst of our pain we can hold a promise. It means that no waiting will ever leave us wanting for a hope that's out of reach. Hope ushers us into a different kind of intimacy with God, where we find peace. Hope expects miracles in the face of uncertainty. Hope creates a new picture from the shattered pieces of what has been broken in the past. For me, hope sat in a mostly empty room in the upper left corner of our house and called it "the nursery."

CHAPTER 16

BEAUTIFUL

CHOOSING TO SEE WHAT IS GOOD

*Remember, you are held safe. You are loved. You
are protected. You are in communion with God
and with those whom God has sent you. What
is of God will last. It belongs to the eternal life.
Choose it, and it will be yours.*
—Henri Nouwen

I sat beneath the turquoise ceiling of Grand Central Terminal,
watching the people of New York from the restaurant above
the main floor and sipping an Arnold Palmer. Predictably, most
people were dressed in black and walking briskly in every direction like an upset ant farm. Some tourists were taking advantage

of the photo opportunity, no doubt surprised by the grandeur and stunning beauty of the train station. I couldn't blame them. The magnitude of the building and the attention to detail in the design still captivated my attention every time I passed through. A choir tested their sound in the acoustics of the large space, adding to the ambiance of my people-watching experience.

The choir continued their set of songs on the main floor below, but songs from the Broadway musical *Beautiful: The Carole King Story*, which I had just seen, were still playing strong in my head. *Beautiful* tells the tale of Carole King's storied career, from being a hit songwriter with her husband Gerry Goffin to becoming one of the most famed solo acts in popular music history. The show also reveals her personal triumphs and struggles, giving the audience a glimpse of her friendship with fellow writers Cynthia Weil and Barry Mann, and her loving, but in many ways tragic, relationship with Gerry. The heartbeat of the show kept time with the beloved, familiar songs she played from her upright piano: "Will You Love Me Tomorrow?," "So Far Away," and "You've Got a Friend"—songs that tell timeless truths.

There were many reasons this musical was my favorite to date. Of course, I knew Carole only from the way her character was portrayed on stage, but she seemed like an old soul like me, and her tenacity, both professionally and personally, resonated deeply with me. She appeared to have the ability to appreciate herself in a culture that often celebrated things that were different from the person she was. I admired her personal security in a volatile industry. I loved the poignant messages that she and Gerry somehow managed to wrap in a three-minute song.

But the words that stayed with me even after the show came from one of the opening lines of the musical. "The funny thing about life is that sometimes it goes the way you want and sometimes it doesn't. And sometimes when it doesn't, you find something beautiful," the actress playing Carole King said.[1]

Holding that line up to the light, I could see the many ways in which her words had been proven true in my own life.

Most of the pain I had experienced in life was related to my identity—feeling unworthy or inadequate. But this recent season had introduced a new kind of pain: the pain of feeling unsafe. My story in this latest chapter had made it quite clear that I was not in control, and in many ways I felt powerless to shape my life into something I could be excited about. I worried that the good in my life would always look like what is good *for* me—like broccoli on a dinner plate—rather than what I might actually *experience* as good.

But as Carole King rightly pointed out, beauty isn't limited to our perfect plans. Even in the wake of a turn we never meant to take, or in the rubble of what's been shattered, we can find beauty. But we cannot find what we refuse to look for. We must be willing to do the challenging but worthy work of committing to see what is good. The difficult thing about feeling unsafe is that the truth can be harder to access. Sometimes life *is* unsafe.

THE RESTORATION THERAPY MODEL THAT GUIDES my work as a therapist outlines three truths we can hold in the midst of uncertain circumstances that leave us feeling powerless and unsafe. First, if we have to go through pain, we have the opportunity to realize what we can take from it and how we can grow through what we go through, carrying the new growth into the future. Second, we may not be able to control everything, but we are not completely powerless. Lastly, even in the bleakest of circumstances, we are not alone.

I have walked countless clients through these ideas—people who found themselves in all kinds of painful and tragic situations such as divorce, the loss of a loved one, and financial insecurity. It is always difficult to recognize the truths as a map for yourself, but they can be a guide that will lead you toward seeing the goodness in your past, present, and future.

This exercise of looking upon the pain of the past and searching for the growth and goodness to carry with us into the future isn't about making a painful thing good. It means carefully taking the pain out of whatever box we would prefer to keep it in, examining it from all sides, and being willing to let the pain be real and the beauty emerge, simultaneously. It's putting our experiences through a sifter and letting go of what's been proven false or unhelpful and taking the treasures that remain with us into the future to be used for good.

Choosing to see what is good in the present requires recognizing that while we cannot control everything, we are empowered to do *some* things. The concept of empowerment is a helpful one, as it distinguishes between what we would like to control and cannot, and what we are actually able to do. It's the idea that no matter what my life looks like right now and no matter what it will look like in the future, I can make choices about what is working for me and what is not.

We can make decisions about with whom we spend our time and with whom we choose to share the deepest and most honest parts of our hearts. We are empowered to say no and empowered to say yes and to give those yeses to what we feel called to do instead of merely to what we feel we should do. We can decide what our priorities are and make decisions that support those priorities. We are empowered to rest before the work is done. We may feel frustrated at times that other people's choices are outside of our control—especially when they are unhealthy or even hurtful to us. We can't control others, but we do get to decide whether we cooperate with the unhealthiness. Giving ourselves permission to make choices allows us to see what is no longer working and what we need more of.

I DECIDED RIGHT THERE in the bustling Grand Central Terminal that there were elements of the past I didn't want to leave behind. More specifically, I wanted to look for the treasure in the wake of what I have lost. At first I saw nothing. And then the light began to peek through the cracks of what had been broken. The formulas that told me that my performance made me more safe and loved had failed and been replaced by faith.

My misconceived ideas about the character of God fell away, and I discovered a new relationship with Him—a relationship characterized by unfiltered trust and an intimacy with my Creator. New friends were brought into my life—even now, it feels impossible to describe these relationships and the weight of what we have carried together. I have a marriage that reminds me a bit of a rock that's been rubbed shiny and smooth by the pressure of waves and sand. I would choose Jimmy in any story.

I am different too. I am far from all fixed-up and fine. But I am a woman who knows hope and chooses courage. I still love hard and am less fearful of failure than I was before. I can look at broken pieces and see possibility. I can view my pain and be curious and maybe even a little bit excited about God revealing His plans, which are so different from my own. I choose to surrender, knowing His ways are better. And mostly, and imperfectly, I am less focused on knowing where I am going and more focused on knowing God.

I also decided that I needed to have more fun. I was managing burnout and flirting with depression, and I needed to make a choice to have fun whether the work was done or not. Fun was a matter of necessity.

You can make these choices too. What you'll need might surprise you. Making choices that allow you to see what is good in the present doesn't simply require the time to notice or the patience for the perfect opportunity to come. It requires courage. We need ears to hear God's guiding voice in our lives and the courage to listen and follow His leading, knowing that it will likely look different than it does in other people's lives. Listening requires courage because it means trusting that God's ways are more beautiful than what is attractive to us. It means remembering that God is more committed to my good than I am.

LIKE ADAM AND EVE IN THE GARDEN, sometimes we forget that we can trust God. I hear the lie of the serpent in the garden of Eden echoed in the fears that can easily haunt my own heart. Eve took a bite of the fruit from the Tree of Knowledge of Good and Evil and sin entered the world, not because Adam and Eve decided to be evil but because they trusted their own will over God's ways. The serpent did not attack Adam and Eve. He merely planted doubt—doubt about the goodness of God's character and uncertainty that God had their best interests at heart. And Adam and Eve's own will became more attractive than the beauty of God's ways. They chose to believe the lie over the Love. Following God's voice and making an empowered choice means choosing to believe the Love.

MY DEPARTURE TIME WAS FAST APPROACHING. As I quickly made my way to track 30 to board my Connecticut-bound train, I spotted a tiny cross etched into the tile walls of the terminal. Its mark had faded with time and was barely noticeable, but it managed to catch my attention as I hurried past. I remembered that God answered Adam and Eve's doubts the same way He has answered ours. We need not look further than the cross for certainty that God loves us and is dedicated to our good. If we truly absorb the magnitude of Christ's sacrifice in our place, we cannot help but stand in awe of God's goodness. Even in the midst of life not feeling good, we can choose to see the cross—God's ultimate gift to us.

The train jumped to a start and lugged forward. As we rumbled past the neon signs of diners, lamp-lit bistros, and shops long closed, I considered what it would look like to make a choice to see what is good about the future. I have no idea what joys and pains await me in my life—this reality alone can spark feelings of being unsafe and powerless. But this is what I do know: no matter what happens, I am not ever going to be alone.

I can't say with confidence what the future will bring. Neither can you. But I have a husband who weathers every kind of day with me. I have a family and close friends who have known me for years, who pray with me and love me across state lines. And I have a strong community in Connecticut that is committed to holding one another in both joy and sorrow. Most reliably,

I have the presence and comfort of the Holy Spirit. And if you know Jesus, you do too. Here, there is goodness and the future is bright—not free of challenge, but free.

When we struggle to see the future as something beautiful to behold, we can remember that God's faithfulness in the past is our hope for today and our courage for tomorrow. I've seen Him move. You've seen Him move. And we are going to stand on uncertain ground with certain faith that He can do it again.

Nearing home, rolling past the more familiar landmarks of my everyday life, I suddenly felt as if I were at a fork in the road, staring at the decade that lay ahead of me. Certainly there were some choices I could make that would shape what would happen in those next ten years, but the biggest choice I saw before me was what I chose to see. I could either spend those years seeing what wasn't and pining after what I wished to be, or I could choose to see what is good about what is.

No matter what might happen, I had choices in how I felt in those years. This doesn't mean we don't grieve the losses. It just means that we don't throw out the gifts in our grief. My life is happening right now. Your life is happening right now. And we get to choose how we see it.

CHAPTER 17

THE GOOD STUFF

CHOOSING INTERDEPENDENCE

We do not love each other without
changing each other.

—Madeleine L'Engle

The coffee shop closed promptly at 6:00 p.m., but as the director of coffee at Espresso NEAT, our friend Kyle had received permission from the owner for our small group to meet in the shop after hours.

I'd come to see Espresso NEAT as a special establishment — the kind of place that holds the soul of a town. As a result, it is a favorite place for people to gather and, for a moment, find joy. You can count on two things when you come to Espresso NEAT:

artfully crafted coffee drinks that look as if they require some kind of degree to make, and always running into a familiar face. Everything about the shop says "Welcome!" and honest conversation, comfortable friendship, and intentional community make sense within its walls.

This coffee shop has played host to some of my most special memories since moving to Connecticut. The two-top table in the corner by the window is where Paige had slipped her and Kyle's wedding invitation across my line of vision when she hardly knew me at all. On the bench just outside the shop door, I sat with my friend Susan as she named gifts in me that I struggled to see in myself at the time. I sipped champagne with friends and sampled our friend Adam's famous barbecue spread as we celebrated Kyle's thirtieth birthday one evening after the shop closed.

I could see now that all these memories had extended a hand, inviting me to a different way of living.

For most of my life, I was mostly an individual sports kind of girl. This was true both in athletics and life. As a swimmer and a runner, I enjoyed athletic competition absent of any form of interdependence. And in life, I was wildly uncomfortable in the vulnerable position of having to depend on others for my success or stability. Accepting the help I needed or wanted meant accepting the notion that I wasn't good enough on my own. In turn, I was also pained by the possibility of letting someone down. Fierce independence provided a false protection against my mistakes potentially hurting someone else. A culture that views feelings as liabilities and applauds brave faces had taught me that strength looked like invulnerability, so I learned to depend on no one but myself.

The wedding invitation, the affirmations Susan spoke over

me on the bench, a group celebration of someone we loved—all these events interrupted my independence and gave me an experience of what life in community might look like if I was willing to live differently.

Paige was right about her prediction four years prior. We did become great friends. It did not take us long to find two other couples and form a small group. This group, the Small Group, is made up of the friends who, over years of shared experiences and prayers, have turned into family. These are the people with whom there is no such thing as calling too late. These are the people who celebrate big when you experience a win and cry alongside you through a painful loss. These are the people who love you enough to always tell you the truth about the gifts they see in you and the ways in which a challenge in your life might be asking you to grow.

We met every other week on Friday nights for four years. So on this particular night at Espresso NEAT, we had all agreed to meet at 6:30 p.m. with our takeout food of choice. Some of us came with tacos, and some came with Thai food. We entered through the back door, each commenting on the novelty of being in this beloved space after hours, just the eight of us. I think we all shared the sentiment that this was a sacred moment in terms of both space and time, as we gathered all together for the last time before Adam and Kelley and their two precious boys moved to Texas.

We made small talk as we settled around an enormous square metal table in the far corner of the shop, one couple to each side. A large-paned window framed a thunderstorm that raged and rolled outside. Inside, the air was thick. Nobody wanted to acknowledge the reality of the goodbye. Nobody wanted to be the first to put words to the finality of a season that was special and transformational for each of us.

We cried as we told each other directly and specifically what we had learned from one another and how each relationship had challenged us to personally grow. We marveled at the fact that every one of us had faced some of the most intense challenges of our lives right after this group was formed. It was as if God had brought us together specifically for a season in which He knew we would need each other. This collective season included marital struggles, mental health battles, infertility, and pregnancy loss. We weathered all of it, and we did it together. And we learned that, actually, there really is no other way.

As a group, we declared certain things to be true and sacred in a world that largely dismisses the value of community and relational intimacy. We decided that life is a team sport, not an individual sport, and that we do not exist just for ourselves; we exist for each other. We believe that because we are created for relationship with God and with others, deep friendship with one another is one of God's greatest gifts to us and well worth the investment. We experienced the truth that when we give one another invitations into our lives—even the dark and messy rooms that we have been taught are best kept with doors shut—we give other people permission to do the same. Together, we learned firsthand that bearing witness to others' transformation also changes something in us.

Not one of us was able to fix or change a single thing about the others' circumstances. There was absolutely nothing we could do to provide a shortcut for navigating the pain that life had hurled in each of our directions. No, being together didn't fix the pain, but it did change the pain. When life felt unsafe, we knew we were not alone. We held one another's hands and said, "I am so sorry about this pain. We are going to get through this together. And I promise that what awaits you on the other side is beautiful."

We learned that pain is always accompanied by a choice. We can either adopt the lies it tells us, or we can stuff our pockets with all the learning that springs from pain and grow from it. As a group, we were committed to seeing each other to that place of growth and redemption no matter how long we had to wait for it. Together we claimed the truth that knowing Christ makes all the difference in our lives. As much as we loved and supported one another, not one of us could offer the wholeness of Christ to the others. So we did our best to point each other back to Him.

We spent the last moments of that final evening affirming the gifts we saw in each other. Kelley's gentleness and brave truth-telling always left me feeling simultaneously comforted and challenged. Adam's strong convictions and warm smile provided a steady presence in our group. It is also worth noting that both Adam and Kelley had amazing gifts in the kitchen, and our group was better, and heavier, for it. Kyle's kind and quiet humility brought peace and perspective in the midst of a challenging week. Paige's quirky sense of humor left us in stitches, and her faithful friendship was a comfort we could all count on. Peter's thoughtful wisdom and strong leadership edified each of us. Lindsay had the gift of hospitality in both her home and her heart and was always a safe place to land. She was fiercely protective of those she loves, and we were grateful to be hers.

The group affirmed Jimmy's ability to connect with all different types of people and love each of them well. And they encouraged me by reflecting on the growth they had seen in my willingness to be vulnerable about how God is challenging me and shaping me in the midst of both joy and pain. When I encountered struggle, this group provided a space where no feelings were off limits and where I felt free to share even the most difficult and unpleasant feelings with God and with them. With the exception of a few relationships in my childhood and in my college years, for the first time in my life, I stepped off the stage and released my worries about whether or not people were clapping.

These seven people loved with a bold love that was not afraid of the dark. And it worked to help heal all of us.

IN 1 CORINTHIANS 12, Paul wrote that each of us has been given a unique gift to reveal to us a part of who God is: "There are different kinds of gifts, but the same Spirit distributes them" (v. 4 NIV).

With Christ in us, and through the power of the Holy Spirit, when we offer our gifts to each other, we display a piece of Christ's identity. Each of our gifts finds its full meaning and value in relationship with one another and sings in concert with others' giftings. Here, community is essential because not one of us can provide a complete picture of the character and power of Christ on our own. Christ can be seen clearly only in the context of community.

This is why we gather in community: when every gift shows up, we begin to understand all the ways Christ shows up for us.

Our small group was a team that knew how to bring our gifts and show up for one another. We had celebrated milestone birthdays and talked around the dinner table until the food grew cold. On multiple occasions, we had gathered to specifically pray for personal situations that looked hopeless through the lens of our human eyes. Together, we had faith that no matter what the view looked like from where we stood, with Jesus there is always something beautiful beyond what we can see. We bounced each other's babies and committed as a group that if it really does take a village to raise a child, we were going to be that village for each other. But one of the qualities I loved most about this group was our ability to honor and care for multiple feelings at the same time.

JUST DAYS BEFORE OUR GROUP'S final gathering, Lindsay had invited me over for lunch. As soon as I arrived, I read anxiety on her face. We had only begun to sit when she told me that she had some news. "I'm pregnant," she said with tears in her eyes and about as much enthusiasm as one would have anticipating a root canal. She was excited, but she had walked each miscarriage and every negative pregnancy test with me, and she was trying to protect me from her joy, fearing that it would cause me more pain.

Her news did sting a little. But the mere thought of not being in the thick of the details of this joy in her life was far more painful. I walked over to her side of the table, hugged her tight, and said, "You can feel excited and I can grieve, but I think it would be better if we could do both together." And that's exactly what we did. I got giddy over all things pink alongside her, and she cried with each passing month of waiting with me.

We do all sorts of things when we are in pain. A common tendency is to assume that no one gets it—that no one understands because no one has experienced what we are going through. This mentality can create a division between loved ones and ourselves.

Though isolating is not my typical response when I am hurt, I found myself fighting the urge to withdraw, assuming that no one could possibly understand what I was going through. I also fought against the tendency to rate my pain against someone else's—to say that I have it worse than everyone else.

I made a choice and a conscious effort to combat these tendencies because I knew this was not truth. After all, Jesus promises we will have trouble. He doesn't say we might have trouble, and He doesn't say only a few of us will experience it. Though pain may come to us in a variety of forms, all humans know suffering. It is a part of being human. And because we are made in the image of a triune, relational God, we are made for relationship. This is a part of being human too.

Our little group of eight had seen more life than we knew could be lived in just four years. It had been a season of both intense joy and heartache. Doing both together had made all the difference.

To commemorate our final gathering, we ended this special evening at Espresso NEAT with a coffee tasting, compliments of Kyle. Another strong conviction that we shared as a group was that Kyle is the best coffee grower, roaster, and brewer there is. On this particular evening, he had just installed an impressive new piece of equipment in the shop. I could not tell you the name of this complicated contraption, but it looked like it belonged on a spaceship and could take flight at a moment's notice. Kyle was eager to show us how it worked, and we were more than willing to receive whatever it produced.

As piping-hot white porcelain mugs of coffee were passed around the group, I reflected on the gift of these relationships in my life. This group had turned me into a team-sports kind of girl, and I was never going back. I wanted to be the kind of person who prioritizes people over projects. I wanted to be someone who participates instead of isolates. And I wanted to forego independence in favor of intimacy. From now on, I wanted to choose interdependence.

There is risk involved with deep relationships. But as I'm learning in so many areas of my life, playing it safe only keeps us dangerously distant from what is truly good. It's better here. Showing up with your messy, honest self and making life a team sport will always be worth it.

I was the last to be served. Kyle leaned over the counter and handed me a taste of Colombia's finest as he smiled proudly and said, "*This* is the good stuff."

As I looked at this shop full of friends, I couldn't contain my smile. *The good stuff indeed.*

CHAPTER 18

A TOTAL ECLIPSE

CHOOSING TRUTH

In darkness God's truth shines most clear.
—Corrie ten Boom

On August 21, 2017, the light of the sun was obscured by the intervention of the moon, casting darkness across a section of the earth in the middle of the day. This particular eclipse was visible in a band that spanned the entire contiguous United States, the path of totality touching fourteen states. The solar event captured the attention and excitement of Americans from all over the country. Many planned vacations and gathered with loved ones for the event, taking pictures in the goofy glasses that had to be worn to protect one's eyes. It was difficult to step into a shop or restaurant without hearing Bonnie Tyler crooning, "A Total Eclipse of the Heart." It was a day referred to by many as the Great American Eclipse.

I would remember it as the day we lost our fourth unborn baby to miscarriage.

Connecticut was not included in the path of totality and was therefore not an ideal destination for enjoying the full eclipse experience. Nevertheless, there was a distinct grayish quality to the light. Staring out my front window felt like looking at a photograph from the seventies. The colors were there, but a hazy filter hid their true hue. It was as if someone dimmed the lights on a clear, sunny day, making what should have been a bright afternoon appear dull instead—a perfect metaphor for our reality. What should have been was not.

The mere fact that this pregnancy was a surprise and came to us without effort had felt like a wink and a smile from God— assurance that this pregnancy was meant to be. Applying human logic and understanding to the mystery of God, it seemed fitting that a surprise pregnancy would yield a baby we would get to meet and know. The cruelty of the circumstantial tease didn't match what I knew to be true about the good character of God.

The emotions that accompanied this fourth loss were not unlike the emotions we had experienced with the other three miscarriages. But admittedly, there was a cumulative impact. Like a boxer rising from the tenth blow to the head, I was slower to stand, more hesitant to believe, and less willing to trust the truth of what I knew. Sometimes pain of any kind can resurrect the feelings that are most familiar to us—even when they don't seem to fit the circumstances. Your most painful wounds—the ones you return to again and again—surface regardless of reason.

Like the shadow that stretched across the United States that day, my feelings felt more real than the truth. They were strong and tenacious in their efforts to make me believe that I was inadequate and that hope was attached only to my circumstances—a treasure that I would search for in vain. These familiar messages worked to convince me that my current situation was a comment on my personal value—that I was unworthy of holding the deepest desires of my heart in my hands. The pain was difficult to ignore.

It was tempting to turn down the volume on how I felt by employing my usual coping strategies. I recognized that now would be the time that I would typically turn to shame, performance, or control. But I was learning for myself what I had always known to be true for my clients: these protective behaviors ultimately serve as a barrier to healing. You can't address the feelings with a reaction.

I sipped my iced, fully caffeinated coffee by the front window of our house and watched neighbors strolling by and squinting at the sky as the eclipse dimmed the day's light. People throughout the country were watching for the darkness, while I was beating back my own. What I knew to be true was being eclipsed by how I felt. It is often easier to believe what we can see. It is tempting to trust what we feel over what we know.

The next day was as bright as it should have been. The daytime hours maintained their light and dwindled with the setting of the sun in the evening. Photos and stories continued to appear from around the country, but people's lives had mostly returned to their normal expectations and rhythms. But I was still caught between the glory and the grief, trying to understand how the two fit together.

THE TENSION BETWEEN feeling and truth makes me think of Peter as he walked toward Jesus on the surface of the churning water (Matthew 14:22–33). He had asked Jesus to command him to "come" (v. 29) if He were truly his Lord and not a ghost. Jesus beckoned Peter to walk toward Him on the waves. Eyes fixed on the reality of Jesus' lordship and the truth of His words, Peter walked, defying the laws of nature and staying afloat. But when he shifted his focus to the strength of the storm, he began to sink. He was caught between the fear of the storm and the faithfulness of Jesus. But when his eyes moved from Jesus, the storm felt more real than the Savior. The darkness overshadowed his faith.

I, too, knew what it was like to be caught between my own fear and God's faithfulness—to let the feelings be more real to me than the truth. I turned on the news in search of the eclipse's more dramatic effects from different parts of the country from the day before. The anticipation captured in the footage was palpable even from the other side of my television screen. The squeals of thrill uttered by those in the path of totality were contagious. As I listened to the enthusiastic reporting and the excitement of America captured in this moment on my television, I had to smile. Even in the darkness, our God's glory shines bright.

I wonder how Peter felt on the day after Jesus pulled him from the waves. Never had it been clearer that Jesus was his Lord and Savior. The facts were clear and the truth was evident, but I can't help but wonder about Peter's feelings after his experience of stumbling upon the water. Did he feel unsafe as he sat in fear of the next storm? Did he shame himself over his inadequacy and weakness in that moment on the waves? Was he frustrated over his powerlessness to stay afloat on his own? Was it still a struggle to trust the power of Jesus over the impact of the storm? Was the terror more real than the glory?

I MOVED ABOUT MY HOUSE, rearranging clutter, trying to extract comfort from mundane tasks. My whole body ached—still pulsing from the emotional impact of the news of our fourth lost heartbeat from the day before. The feelings remained both real and raw. A family felt like a gift that would never have my name on it. I fought the urge to turn my anger inward, allowing shame to search for a reason I was not good enough for this dream. The future felt unsafe—a vehicle for more disappointment. Trusting the truth over how I felt would have to be a choice—a decision that requires effort.

I am at my core a feelings person. I am comfortable sharing my feelings with others. I have chosen a career that gives me the privilege of helping others understand and address their feelings. My favorite ingredient in any conversation is feelings. I believe emotions give us valuable information about why we have the tendency to react the way we do. Feelings should be honored and given a voice. Still, like the storm that threatened Peter, the feelings we carry are real, and they're worth listening to—but they don't always tell us the truth about our identity and safety.

The feelings that accompanied my grief over our loss were real, but they were not true. There is a profound difference between feeling inadequate and being inadequate—between failing and *being* a failure. Pain is a breeding ground for lies to grow, but we get to decide whether we will agree with them. This distinction between feeling and truth exists with all our emotions, and every feeling offers the opportunity to choose between them. The cross is what distinguishes the two. Because of what Jesus accomplished through His death and resurrection, we can make a mistake without becoming a mistake. Even in the midst of honoring my grief, I saw for myself a clear choice. I could choose to believe what felt real, or I could answer the facts and my feelings with faith in what I knew to be true, regardless of my circumstances.

The same choice is available to you. As Peter discovered when he walked on water in the midst of the storm, it is easy to take more notice of what we feel than what we know to be true of God's character and power. The reality of the storm tempts us to shift our focus from our Savior. If we wait to feel peace before we are willing to trust the Source of peace, we will wait in fear of the next wave. As long as our peace and joy are dependent on our feelings, we will only ever experience the shallow thrill of circumstantial peace and joy.

Reflecting once again on the natural phenomenon of the day before, it occurred to me that the thrill of the eclipse was in knowing that though the light was gone, the source of the light was not. No one believed that the sun had vanished. No one worried that the world would never see light again. The eclipse obscured the light, but it did not eliminate it. And even the experience of darkness was a reflection of God's bright glory.

With the loss of yet another baby I would not know this side of heaven, the light was difficult to access. I did not feel peace. I did not feel joy. I felt a lot like how I imagined Peter felt in the days that followed his rescue from the storm. I felt fearful of another miscarriage and even more afraid that my story would look unrecognizably different from the one I desired. I wondered if I would ever see light—if peace and joy would ever be my reality.

But in the midst of my real feelings, I knew that the light was not gone. Because of Jesus, I knew that darkness is temporary. Life may not feel happy, but we can know joy. Life may not feel calm, but we can know peace. And even the darkest seasons in our lives do not change the truth of God's goodness. The truth of God's love and sovereignty are truer than what feels real right now.

Our emotions are often understandable and can be very convincing, but we have a choice in the message we carry forward. When the feelings confront us, we can agree or we can gently address them with the truth. The messages we give to ourselves—spoken or unspoken—matter because we listen to ourselves more than we listen to anyone else. No voice is louder than the one inside our own head. Therefore, the message we give this voice has a profound impact on how we interact with ourselves and others as we move forward. I used to think that trusting the truth meant ignoring or denying our feelings. But we cannot speak truth until we are honest about the lies we are speaking to.

Pausing from my feeble attempts to remove a stubborn stain from our carpet, I held my face in my hands. I made a living helping people trust the truth, and yet it always amazed me how difficult it could be when it was my turn to do the same. But I knew that peace and joy were gifts that were available for me to open even now, if I was willing to choose the truth in this moment.

Tears stung my dry eyes as I said the words out loud in the midst of the pain.

"I know that my painful circumstances are not a reflection of my value. I am precious to God.

"I know that God sees and cares deeply that my heart is broken.

"I know that I am safe in God's economy.

"I know that God is good, and He is actively moving in my life.

"I know that God has the whole picture, and I only have a piece.

"I know that this pain will not be wasted.

"I know that I have the comfort of the Holy Spirit available to me. I am not alone.

"I know that the Savior is more powerful than the storm.

"I know that even in the darkness, God's glory shines bright.

"I know this is the truth, and I choose to believe it."

CHAPTER 19

HOW SWEET IT IS

CHOOSING TO PARTNER

> *What marriage is for: It is a way for two spiritual friends to help each other on their journey to become the persons God designed them to be.*
>
> —TIMOTHY KELLER AND KATHY KELLER

Connecticut in July is delicious. After eight months of wearing my knee-length parka as a daily uniform, it felt like a treat to walk outside without wearing so much as a light sweater in the evenings when the fireflies are thick on the breeze. The local produce seemed to come into season all at once as roadside stands and farmers markets boasted buckets of berries and ripe, fuzzy peaches. American flags flew everywhere from bridges to flower pots. The beaches along the Long Island shore were peppered with brightly colored beach umbrellas and Northeasterners who had taken time to pause and actually enjoy the lives they worked so hard for.

One of the curious things about living in Fairfield County is life's rhythm in the summer. Until the move, I had never lived in a place where the scheduled pace of life during the school-year months stood in such stark contrast to the pace people kept in the summer months. July marked the beginning of "slow," which meant fewer expectations and scheduled activities. Some people disappeared for the entire summer, checking out of their routine for a solid eight weeks.

The Fourth of July holiday is also unique in Fairfield County because most of the festivities, including the town's firework show, do not actually take place on the Fourth of July. We are told this is due to the need to share fire departments and to keep the beaches open on the holiday itself, but I'm not sure anybody really knows. As a result, people tend to celebrate on July 2 or 5, but rarely on the fourth. My neighbor calls this the "faux fourth."

On the actual Fourth of July, Jimmy and I decided to leave town and drive to Lenox, Massachusetts, for a day in the Berkshires and an evening of being serenaded by James Taylor at a concert venue called Tanglewood. The day had one goal: to reconnect. Our marriage had weathered a lot of life in five years. Jimmy had been my constant companion and steadfast supporter. He loved his job more and more and felt constantly affirmed in our decision to leave our California life to move across the country. Though we had both experienced great success in our careers and now felt closely connected to our community here, Jimmy was keenly aware that the transition to the East Coast had been more difficult for me.

Also, navigating infertility and pregnancy loss had made the past couple of years particularly challenging. Hoping, praying, grieving, and doing what little we could do to become parents had been painful for both of us in different ways. Our reality left me feeling inadequate and alone. Jimmy, in turn, felt powerless and defective. We knew we loved one another, but the pain of this past year was like a fog that made it difficult to see each other as anything but an enemy.

Pain has a way of making us selfish to the point that our hurt and personal desires are all that matter. We become myopic about our own dreams and worries, and it is very difficult to see through our own perspective to another's point of view.

The move to Connecticut had exposed my brand of brokenness in ways I was not proud of. The feelings I had experienced in its wake left me keeping score—laser-focused on everything I had sacrificed and suffered through to start a new life on the East Coast. I found myself being self-righteous, resentful, and destructively entitled, taking control and turning "us" decisions into "me" decisions. I never actually acted independently from Jimmy in these choices, but I felt strongly that I had the right to do things my way when it came to decisions ranging from making purchases to making medical decisions around our infertility diagnosis.

The pain of transition and of questioning whether I would ever be a mom—and on my worst days wondering whether there was a reason I wasn't good enough to be a mom—resurrected old conversations. I wielded weapons that should have been laid down long ago. An expert in Jimmy's weaknesses and unwilling to acknowledge his strengths, I was blind to the fact that I wasn't married to the enemy but to a person who was in excruciating pain too. We were two people drowning in our feelings and hurting each other in our attempts to survive.

The getaway to the Berkshires was about recalling all the reasons we chose each other. We needed to remember that our relationship was more than the pain we shared and that our relationship was worth celebrating in the midst of our grief over not being parents. We needed to remember that even though we felt like characters in a tragedy, we were living a love story too. We needed to sincerely apologize to each other for the words we had spoken from our pain that had accidentally hurt each other—and the words that were fired to *intentionally* hurt each other. It was time to take responsibility for the ways in which we each needed to grow and have the courage to walk toward each other differently—to remember that we are on the same team and start acting like the partners we had forgotten we were.

As we drove the tree-lined, winding Massachusetts roads, Jimmy at the wheel and my bare feet up on the dashboard, I pictured our wedding day. Even five years later, I could watch the day play in my memory like a movie. I remembered every detail and fluttering feeling. We were married at the Adamson House—a Spanish-style venue just down the street from Pepperdine University, where we met as students. The day started at 6:00 a.m., an hour I rarely witnessed. I was unable to sleep, so I spent some time watching the sun wake up the day on the back porch. I had only been outside a few minutes when my dad stepped out onto the porch, looked at me, and then burst into tears. I am sure I will remember that hug for the rest of my life.

I remembered how I felt in my lace dress. I could see the citrus fruit peeking from the warm-colored floral arrangements. And I'll never forget the feeling in my stomach when I rounded the corner and saw Jimmy at the end of the aisle. He had asked our pastor to remind him to absorb the moment by taking a mental picture as I made my way toward him—a request Jimmy quickly regretted, as he did not stop crying for the rest of the ceremony, which I kind of loved.

I remembered our first dance, chatting and smiling as we danced to James Taylor's "How Sweet It Is." I could visualize the dance floor—full until the moment we left. I remembered giggling as we ran toward the old-fashioned getaway car at the end of the evening. Because of California's fire hazards, we were not permitted to light sparklers, so we borrowed a friend's idea and settled for glow sticks instead. For some reason, people felt the urge to throw them at us as we ran along the path toward the car, but we were having too much fun to care.

As the car climbed higher into the Berkshire mountains, I thought about the expectations I wore like an accessory on my wedding day. Though I knew a lot of the right answers when it came to relationships, there was a large part of my heart that believed that marriage would be it—the crowning gift or achievement that would allow me to never want for anything else again.

I started dating much later than most of my girlfriends and, after a while, I found myself longing to be in a relationship and panicking that I wasn't, questioning my worth in the absence of any kind of romance in my life. I believed that I was only interesting to the extent that someone else was interested in me. And like so many things we long for, it became the hinge for my identity and sense of security. The intoxicating syndrome isn't limited to romantic relationships. Perhaps you've danced this same dance with the need to be a particular friend's favorite or the desire to win the approval of a mentor or boss.

My value and sense of safety swung up and down with my situation. I was under the impression that marriage could deliver on promises that I now knew couldn't be kept. I pictured feeling confident and secure, as if knowing that someone I loved loved me would be enough. I expected this to serve as a shield against pain—as if life couldn't hurt me in the same ways it had before. Perhaps love from someone else would make up for the ways it was hard to love myself, and maybe it would even rescue me from having to do the hard work of learning how to love myself. But this kind of fulfillment is a promise that even the best gifts in life cannot deliver.

The change and the loss we had encountered in our short life together had exposed these ideas as frauds, and we could no longer proceed with these same expectations. If our only strategy was to add time to our current method of operation, the unrealistic expectations we shared and the distance between the two of us would be more difficult to overcome.

THE REALITY THAT WE CANNOT MEET EACH OTHER'S NEEDS changed the way we interacted so that we were neither dependent on nor independent from each other. Instead of feeling desperate to have our needs met by each other and getting angry or resentful when that plan failed, we could reach out to comfort and care for each other, knowing the One who can ultimately meet our needs. Here, we are able to partner and be an *interdependent* team.

We put the relationship above our individual comforts. We

do what is good for the relationship even if that decision looks different from what we would choose on our own. We trust that the relationship is greater than the sum of its parts, and that two people depending on Christ are more connected than two people trying to meet all of each other's needs.

Marriage doesn't provide the only opportunity to partner. At the same time I was moving away from complete dependence and learning to partner in my relationship with Jimmy, I was learning to fight my tendency toward unhealthy independence and in-vulnerability as I slowly began to trust others with my flaws. Any kind of relationship can teach us the importance of give and take, where we neither have to be silent nor be the only voice heard. We can love and be loved deeply and imperfectly while ultimately entrusting our value and security to God.

WHEN WE ARRIVED AT TANGLEWOOD, we selected a few square feet on the crowded lawn to call our own and set up a picnic. There were seats inside a covered open-air stage area, but most attendees had a tradition of setting up a picnic in the hours leading up to the concert. Many stayed on the lawn for the whole evening to enjoy their picnic at their leisure. We quickly understood that our picnic was more like a sack lunch in comparison to the impressive spreads that surrounded our humble blanket—a blanket we had scored for free from an ESPN swag bag.

People from all over the Northeast set up camp, complete with patriotic flower arrangements; red, white, and blue candles placed in candelabras; and place settings complete with bone china and crystal. We enjoyed people-watching until we made our way into the amphitheater, eager to find our seats and hear

James Taylor play in his hometown. It did not take us long to figure out that we were the youngest audience members by at least twenty years, but we didn't care. We are both old souls, and it suited us perfectly.

The lights dimmed, and James Taylor played one hit after another. He told stories and strummed his guitar with a comfort and ease that made you feel like you were sitting on the rug of his living room. We laughed at his jokes and sang along to all the familiar favorites. I had forgotten what it felt like to just have fun with Jimmy.

It was time for the last song, and James was only a few notes in when I looked up excitedly at Jimmy to find him smiling at me as he pulled me into the aisle to dance to "How Sweet It Is." And as we danced, I beamed.

"Sweet" meant something entirely different to me now than it did when we danced to this song five years before. At our wedding, the sweetness was about the joy of finding each other and celebrating the love that we shared. But now, as we danced to the same song five years later, it was apparent to me that the sweetest part of life wasn't simply the love between the two of us but the way our relationship had grown us and ushered us toward the love of Christ. It was a gift to share the pain of this season together—to have a companion in the waiting and in the wrestling. But for the first time, I was able to see that the relationship itself was not the answer to that pain.

When change and loss were added to the love we shared, we quickly realized that the love between the two of us wasn't enough to carry these burdens, which shined the light on our need for Christ in ways we had not yet seen. This was the real sweetness: learning to love each other by pointing one another to a Love that is more powerful than what either one of us can give—a Love that can fulfill.

As we approached our fifth wedding anniversary, we were learning for ourselves that we can love one another deeply, but we do not complete each other. The love that we share is meaningful but not powerful enough to heal the doubts and insecurities we each carry, or fix what someone else broke long ago. Though we shape one another, we are not the source of each other's identity and security. Certainly we are called to love and support one another, but no amount of external affirmation can heal our internal wounds—even if the affirmation is coming from our spouse or someone we care for deeply.

When we said, "I do," we were saying yes to a person, not a plan. When we vowed to love each other for better or for worse, we really had no idea what that would mean for us. We knew the concept in theory, but we had yet to discover what our particular version of that vow would be. We still don't know. But our few years of marriage have taught us that though you get to choose your partner for the adventure, for the most part, you don't get to select the adventure itself.

As the fireworks boomed above us, I rested my head on Jimmy's chest. How sweet it is.

CHAPTER 20

GETTING FOUND

CHOOSING JOY

*I have learned to kiss the waves that throw me up
against the Rock of Ages.*
—CHARLES SPURGEON

It was colder than it should be in April. Even after six years in Connecticut, I hadn't accepted that April is a month that looks more like winter than spring. Espresso NEAT was even more crowded than usual, but I managed to claim a spot at the large metal table by the window, framing the brown lawns, leafless trees, and the stubborn patches of snow and ice that had yet to thaw. Inside, the view was much warmer. The baristas I'd come to know by name were busy perfecting the same beautiful and delicious drinks. Across the room, a friend was putting the final touches on a big project she'd been working on. In the back corner, one of our beloved pastors at Trinity Church was engaged in conversation with a congregant. On the way into the shop, I'd bumped into one of my closest friends, Steph. A hug from her was just the encouragement I needed as I attempted to find the words to leave you with.

On the surface, very little has changed since I wandered into this shop six years ago. Like the weather outside, so much of what I thought would be different by this point has remained very much the same. My heart still has the same fault lines—places that are prone to disappointment and familiar wounds. Jimmy and I have a full community and more established careers but still carry the same longings to grow our family, and, on most days, that future looks uncertain. Though we have prayed and longed for a different picture, we continue to awaken to a scene that mostly looks the same. And despite feeling embraced by our friends here, I still feel like a bit of a misfit on the East Coast.

But digging deeper, past what meets the eye upon first glance, everything has changed. In many ways, the last several years could be characterized by change and loss. I lost tangible things as I experienced transition, failure, loneliness, disappointment, and grief. But in God's graciousness, I also lost the props to my faith—the touch points of security that stabilized my identity and sense of safety. My usual means of feeling valued and protected no longer worked when I confronted pain. The formulas I had been accustomed to using to feel significant failed and left me feeling inadequate. My efforts to control the growth of my family and career only left me feeling powerless. The accomplishments I thought would never cease to bring me joy had only left me feeling empty with time.

I had tried all of my favorite tricks—shaming myself, performing, perfecting my image, proving myself, making attempts to control my life—and every single one had fallen short. When these strategies stopped working, I did turn to God. But I kept Him small at first, keeping Him on the periphery of my agenda. I viewed Him merely as the facilitator of my dreams—the provider of the things in which I had really invested my peace and joy. But as I discovered for myself, adding things to Jesus only makes us feel as if we are never enough and it's never enough. All these strategies had been called out as frauds.

I would never tell you that the pain itself is good or something to be thankful for. I don't believe it's healthy to ignore the dark cloud and force our eyes upon a silver lining. We walk with a God who is both in authority over us as our Creator and right beside us as our Father and Friend. He knows our hurt because He chose to identify with our pain and absorbed it on the cross. He doesn't say all things *are* good; He promises to work them *for* good. And there is a significant difference. Though pain is not a gift, it does give us a gift. When our comforts fail us, we are left with empty hands to receive the One who sustains.

I think this is what Jesus was talking about when He spoke the Beatitudes in the very beginning of His Sermon on the Mount. With each beatitude, He taught us that there is blessing in any story that enflames our longing for Christ. I especially love the way *The Message* version of the Bible articulates what Jesus said about those who mourn: "You're blessed when you feel you've lost what is most dear to you. Only then can you be embraced by the One most dear to you" (Matthew 5:4).

Throughout this season I never stopped believing in God. But in the midst of my challenging circumstances, the pain I felt had allowed me to lose the misconceived ideas I had about Him, placing me in a position where I could get reacquainted with His character—this time, for real. Storms wake us up to truth we would otherwise not see. I don't believe God causes the pain, but I do think He will use it to take our hands off what will ultimately destroy us.

Thinking about my season of struggle, I often ask myself this question: Would I have chosen to keep my comfortable life and carry on with my protected way of living and my small ideas about God, or was it all worth it to be introduced to more of my big God? My story is not over. Moving forward, I am committed to choosing the latter.

This doesn't mean that the loss isn't devastatingly painful. It is. But Jesus' words offer a promise that our deep pain ushers us into a deeper love.

As my fingers were pried off entitlements and the life I thought I wanted was pulled from my grasp, I became free to grab hold of an enduring truth. No longer numb with comfort, I yearned for Christ again. I cried out for help and found my longings answered in the form of the presence and person of Jesus. Losing what I thought I wanted allowed me to find the one thing I need: companionship with Him.

I recently saw a Broadway musical called *Come From Away*. The show tells the powerful story of when the tiny town of Gander, Newfoundland (population nine thousand), hosted six thousand passengers from all over the world as planes were grounded in their small town just after the September 11 attacks. The story carries several poignant themes about our shared experience of being human across cultural divides. But there was one moment that stood out to me as I sat captivated by this story. In one of the final scenes, the passengers return to Gander for the tenth anniversary of September 11 to remember the time they spent together in the terrifying and uncertain days that followed the terrorist attacks. During this scene, one of the passengers faces the audience and says, "Tonight, we honor what we lost. But we also commemorate what we found."[1]

Tragedy forced those thirty-eight planes down on the airstrip of the tiny town of Gander. There was nothing good about the reason this community was brought together. The events of September 11 were beyond horrific, and many of these passengers lost loved ones in the attacks. They returned to one another ten years later to remember what they lost. But they also came back to celebrate what they found. Out of tragedy, they found great joy. Out of the discomfort of cultural divides, they found close community. The pain of loss had allowed them to see which blessings in their lives really mattered. In the middle of the wreckage, they found joy that lasts.

Each of these themes mirrors the rhythm of the cross: out of death springs life—a theme I now recognize in my own life, especially in this latest season. In the midst of the rubble of what has been broken and lost in my own life, I, too, have found a lasting peace and joy.

I used to think that peace and joy were only found during moments in life that could be categorized as happy—as a kind of reward for a job well done, or receiving what I hoped for from life. But I now know that peace and joy can be for everyone right now. With Jesus, they can be chosen and received in any circumstance at any time.

Choosing joy does not protect us from hurt or provide easy answers to our questions. In many ways, sipping my coffee in

Espresso NEAT now, I carry the same wounds in my heart and questions in my mind that I did on the day I first walked into this place. I still wrestle with the pain of knowing that God can but wondering if He will. I still find His timing hurtful sometimes. I still worry that God and I will never agree on what is good. I still wonder about my ability to see the beauty in God's plans.

But I know that in the wake of what I have lost, and in the empty space of unanswered questions, I have found a freeing truth. And these truths are not God's consolation prizes or a second-rate life where our dreams go unfulfilled in the ways we hoped. These are precious lessons—prizes that get revealed and can be fully realized only in the context of painful circumstances.

In a conversation I recently had with my mentors and friends Terry and Sharon, I talked about my grief and longing for a change in particular circumstances in my life. They listened with kindness and comfort before sharing with me some ideas about hope. I'll never forget one of the things they told me: "Hope only gets deployed in times of struggle."

I have decided that I am not thankful for the struggle. But I am grateful and consider myself sincerely blessed to be a woman who knows hope.

None of us is promised an easy life. There is nothing we can do to keep ourselves immune to trials, and we cannot eradicate painful feelings from our lives.

But even the most difficult seasons are not absent of God's love. And this love changes us. This is what I want to tell you: on the far side of pain we don't prefer, we find transformation we wouldn't trade.

Walking this life with Jesus, depending on His strength and

calling on His love, leaves us transformed more into His likeness. Our Father's arms can't help but leave us changed.

I may not know the storyline of my life, but because of Jesus, I can know the conclusion of the story. God's light always pierces through the darkness. As a result, in the midst of my pain I can carry a hope that is bigger than my failures, loneliness, and heartbreak. I am learning that our hope is not in a change of circumstance but in the constant goodness of God. And sometimes the answers to our prayers look nothing like the outcome we have longed for, but rather joy that we absolutely cannot see from where we currently stand.

One might assume that this is my story about finding God, or at least finding more of Him than I knew before. But if any one of us finds God, it is because He found us first. No, this is not my story of finding God. This is my story about a God who did everything to find me.

And He's done the same for you. I envisioned Christ's pursuit of me as a rescue from unwanted circumstances. Sometimes we feel His pursuit in this way—warm, cozy, and close—full of breakthroughs and good news. But now I see that sometimes His mercy looks like the failure of behaviors that were never meant to work. It looks like storms waking us up to truth that would otherwise go unseen. It looks like pain that pries our fingers off what we thought we wanted.

I didn't know I needed rescuing from my own dreams. I had no idea that sometimes the greatest joy is found when we are drained of all misplaced hope and shallow identities. I was blind to the truth that the end of myself is actually the beginning of transformation, where real hope can take root. In what I now recognize to be God's graciousness to me, He gifted me a story that I would have never had the courage to choose for myself—a story that has led me to Him.

Maybe your story is different from mine. Your pain comes from another direction, and different circumstances shaped your wounds. I don't want you to miss the opportunity to examine your own story and find the treasure in the wake of what's been lost in your life—the loss of broken dreams, unmet expectations, or behaviors that have failed you. What are the touch points of security that you've lost along the way? How did you feel about yourself or your circumstances when these securities were taken from you? Maybe you've tried to protect yourself in ways that look similar to how I've reacted to my pain: shame, performance, and control. Perhaps you've guarded yourself with different shields like blame, anger, or a numbing escape.

The diverse faces of these protective behaviors have two things in common: they are all equally relationally destructive, and none of them are effective. In fact, not only are they ineffective but they also guarantee the very pain we are hoping to avoid. As disorienting and painful as it can be when they fail or when we make the brave decision to let them go, we find ourselves open to a transforming truth—truth that changes our relationship with others and ourselves. Here, we recognize that we can hold hope, we can claim peace, and we can dance for joy regardless of our situation or position. Because when the transforming reality of God's grace finds you, you will see that hope, peace, and joy are already yours. They're just waiting to be chosen.

I began to pack up my things before heading home from Espresso NEAT. I glanced up and suddenly saw the life that danced within these walls during the most significant season of my life so far. It felt impossible to ignore the change inside myself since those early, lonely days in Connecticut. And by God's grace, I felt nothing but gratitude. I took the warmth of this space and these memories with me out into the cold, early spring.

I feel thankful for a story I would have never picked and transformation I didn't know to look for. The failure of my idols in the face of my pain had led me to feel lost. But I now know that being lost is just the beginning of getting found.

LOOKING UP DISCUSSION QUESTIONS

1. How does knowing the truth about your significance and security invite you to live differently and make different choices?
2. Regardless of whether your circumstances change, how does God's truth allow you to walk in peace and dance for joy?
3. Describe a time when your circumstances remained unchanged but there was a change in your heart and in your approach to a situation.
4. What is something that you've been hesitant to ask God for because you're afraid you will be disappointed?
5. Knowing you have some empowerment in your life, what are some choices you need to make in your life right now that will help you live more peacefully and joyfully?
6. How have you seen the gifts of your friends or people in your community reflect different ways God shows up for each of us?
7. Describe a time when you were tempted to focus on the storm instead of the Savior.
8. How have you seen God's glory shine bright in the dark (times of uncertainty or pain)?
9. How have you been tempted to look to a relationship (with a spouse, friend, mentor, or another person) to heal your pain or fix what feels broken?
10. Looking back, how has losing what you thought you wanted allowed you to find companionship with Christ?

THANK YOU

This book was a team effort, born out of a community of new friends and old friends breathing life into my story. Without their participation, this story would have remained only in my heart.

I'm thankful for You, Jesus. Thank You for gifting me a story I would have never been brave enough to choose for myself. This is the journey that threw me back into Your arms, and for that, I am grateful. If I have You and nothing else, I have everything. This book is my joyful noise to You.

Love and profound gratitude to my mentors and friends Terry and Sharon Hargrave. It's difficult to find words that capture just how much your encouragement, time, prayers, love, comfort, wisdom, teaching, and discipleship have impacted my heart, my family, and my work. The brilliant model you've developed, restoration therapy, has changed the way I see relationships and significantly shaped the story found within these pages. *Thank you!* I love you both. Terry, thank you for investing so generously in me as a therapist through our consultation time over the past ten years. I am blessed to be "covered in your dust."

To my literary agent and friend, Angela Scheff—I can picture exactly where I was sitting when you said yes to me and this message. Thank you for taking a chance on me and for offering your wisdom and support so freely. I wouldn't want to be in this business with anyone else. You are humble, loving, and brilliant and such a gift to me!

To the kind and capable W Publishing team—I feel so thankful for your talents and intentionality as you helped me think through each element of this book.

Special thanks to my gifted and wise editor, Debbie Wickwire—I would fly to Texas just to hug you and tell you thank you. Thank you for saying yes. Thank you for writing beautiful prayers for me and this book over email to keep me going. You are the salt of the earth, and it is a gift of grace to have the opportunity to work with you.

Tim Schraeder, I've lost count of the number of times I've thanked God for allowing our paths to cross. Thank you for being the calm to my crazy and for working alongside me in the trenches to share this message with as many people as possible. I'm thankful for both your talent and your friendship.

Margot Starbuck, thank you for your constant affirmation of me and my writing, and for championing this message before we knew it would be read by anyone else.

Elisabeth Hasselbeck, your prayers and insights offered me comfort and courage as I lived the story within these pages.

Thank you for reminding me Jesus is always the ultimate gift. I look up to you in a million ways and am so thankful for your willingness to give me your "delightful yes" to partnering with me on this project. I love you and your big heart!

Jess Connolly, I am so inspired by your words. Both your writing and the encouragement you've offered me through our friendship across state lines have blessed me immensely! Your wisdom is a beautiful combination of comfort and challenge, and I am so grateful that God allowed our paths to cross. You are a gift.

Linds, thank you for being such a present friend, praying with me, hugging me tight, and celebrating my joys and grieving my sorrows as if they were your own as I lived and wrote this story. I love you.

Barb, thank you for being such a faithful prayer warrior and cheerleader in my life, reminding me that God has the best plan and for helping me remember to celebrate as that plan unfolds. Thank you for being such a safe and loving person to process with. Goodness, am I grateful for you!

Jeans, you've been so generous to constantly reach back with comfort and wisdom as you helped me navigate this world of writing and publishing (and life!). Thank you for being a constant reminder of God's faithfulness and grace. I treasure both the tears and the laughs we've shared over the years.

Elisabeth S., God knew best when He sent me straight to your doorstep when we moved to Connecticut. I was looking for a counseling job, and God blessed me with a forever-friend instead. I will never stop calling you my "guardian angel."

Berit, I'm still in awe of God's graciousness in blessing our family with the gift of *you*! You've been the best "Tante" to

James and a dear friend to me. Thank you for offering your time, prayers, and wisdom so freely. We love you!

To the Megans—Everyone needs a "Megan" in their life, and God blessed me with two! Both of you have been faithful and loyal soul sisters to me since I was a baby. I love you both! Megan Kelly, thank you for reading early drafts of this proposal and offering both your refining wisdom and enthusiastic encouragement, and for normalizing my writing woes. Megan Dunn, thank you for praying constantly through each leg of both the living and writing of this journey.

To the friends that continuously supported me as I put pen to page to write this book: Adam, Anne, Blair, Brooke, Elena, Kelley, Krista, Kyle, Mike, Paige, Peter, Phoebe, Rachel, Shirley, Steph, Susan A., Susan B., Tori, and Vicky. I'm grateful for each of you!

To our community at Trinity Church—You are our Connecticut family. We love doing life with you. Special thanks to Ben Valentine, who has offered me insight and wisdom that is all over these pages.

Special thanks and so much love to my parents, Chuck and Gigi Wallace. Thank you for providing me with a foundation of love and security and for introducing me to Jesus and showing me the joy of walking this life with Him. I've learned so much from you and am proud and grateful to be your daughter.

To my sisters, Brianna Lillibridge and Laura Anne Bowlin— Mom and Dad raised us to be best friends and that is exactly what we have become. I treasure your love and wisdom in my life. Thank you for being my constant cheerleaders. Riley and Austin—Having brothers is fun! I love you both.

To my beloved in-laws, Jim, Sheri, Nick, Betsy, Elizabeth,

and Shelton—I hit the jackpot with you! Thank you for your faithful prayers, steadfast support, and enthusiastic celebration. Being a part of your family is a gift. Thank you for embracing me and loving me so well.

To Jimmy—How sweet it is to be loved by you. You are the best chapter of my story. Thank you for reminding me to believe in the God who called me when I lost my confidence, for making me laugh when I took myself too seriously, and for being the best friend to me as we live this journey together. I would choose you in any story. I love you with my whole heart.

To James and Charlie—Being your mama is a joy. You are constant reminders of God's lavish love and the fact that all gifts in this life are truly gifts of grace. I love you both so much!

NOTES

Chapter 1: California

1. Terry D. Hargrave and Franz Pfitzer, *Restoration Therapy: Understanding and Guiding Healing in Marriage and Family Therapy* (New York: Routledge, 2011).
2. This poem is often attributed to Sir Francis Drake, but there is some debate about whether he is the author. See Joshua Horn, "Francis Drake's Prayer: Fact or Fiction?," Discerning History (website), November 22, 2014, http://discerninghistory.com /2014/11/francis-drakes-prayer-fact-or-fiction.

Chapter 2: A Heart Divided

1. "Strong's Greek: 3309. merimnaó," Bible Hub, https://biblehub .com/greek/3309.htm.

Chapter 6: Yogis

1. *To Kill a Mockingbird*, playwright Aaron Sorkin, dir. Bartlett Sher, Sam S. Shubert Theatre, New York, NY, March 9, 2019.

Chapter 9: The Ladies Who Lunch

1. I am indebted to my pastor, Ben Valentine, for his teachings on this story, which have influenced my thoughts here.
2. Paul Tillich, *Love, Power, and Justice* (London: Oxford University, 1954).

Chapter 14: Growing

1. This concept was first introduced to me in a sermon by Richard Dahlstrom.
2. Lara Casey, *Cultivate: A Grace-Filled Guide to Growing an Intentional Life* (Nashville: Thomas Nelson, 2017), 49.

Chapter 16: Beautiful

1. *Beautiful: The Carole King Musical*, book by Douglas McGrath, words and music by Gerry Goffin, Carole King, Barry Mann, and Cynthia Weil, Stephen Sondheim Theater, New York, NY, December 15, 2018.

Chapter 20: Getting Found

1. *Come From Away*, book and music by Irene Sankoff and David Hein, Gerald Schoenfeld Theater, New York, NY, March 31, 2018.

ABOUT THE AUTHOR

NICOLE ZASOWSKI is a licensed marriage and family therapist, writer, and speaker based in the state of Connecticut, where she lives with her husband and two young boys. As an old soul who wears her heart proudly on her sleeve, Nicole loves using her words to help others find an enduring peace and joy outside of circumstance.